FREEZER
COCKTAIL

CONTENTS

Introduction vi

The Science of Freezer Cocktails 1

Essential Gear 5

Vodka | 9

Rum | 41

Gin | 63

Agave (Tequila and Mezcal) | 101

Whiskey (Bourbon, Rye and Scotch) | 123

Brandy, Cognac and Vermouth | 161

Acknowledgments 172

Drinks Index 173

Index 175

About the Author 182

INTRODUCTION

What's a freezer cocktail? It works like this: take a full bottle of the primary liquor for your favorite cocktail and pour off just enough to leave room to add the other ingredients needed for it. Cap the bottle, give it a good shake, then store it in the freezer. Ready for a drink? Just pour.

Sure, it's not that difficult to make a cocktail the old-fashioned way: measure out a few shots of liquor, toss in some bitters and ice, give it all a shake or stir, then strain it into a glass. But there are any number of reasons to keep batched bottles of your favorite cocktails on hand. Entertaining is among the most compelling. So is ease. Surely, I'm not alone in having plenty of nights when even a little effort feels like too much.

Liquor companies know this. It's why they have flooded the market with individual canned cocktails, as well as larger, crowd-ready bottled cocktails. Yet most of them are ridiculously bad and outrageously expensive. And if you prefer a particular vermouth in your Martini? You're out of luck.

And so the freezer cocktail.

The idea is so simple and obvious that you might wonder why you need a book of recipes to show you how it's done. But while the preparation is straightforward, there is a bit of science involved—you have to make sure the ingredients in the bottle don't actually freeze. I've done the trial and error for you—sorting out which ingredients can freeze and which can't; scaling up classic recipes so they still taste balanced; accounting for the dilution you'd normally get when shaking and stirring with ice; determining the best way to serve each; and offering single-serve cocktail ideas for using up the extra liquor you pour off.

These batch recipes are pour-and-serve simple. This means that if a cocktail requires an ingredient that doesn't freeze well—such as large volumes of juice or egg whites—I found a delicious workaround. It felt like cheating to create recipes that require further ingredients and mixing after the initial bottling. The exception is cocktails that are finished with something sparkling, such as prosecco or tonic water (bubbles are no fans of the freezer).

This is why some of the recipes in this book may sound a bit different. Take the Cosmopolitan. It typically is made with a high ratio of sweetened cranberry juice. But getting the flavor right requires more juice than can be stored in the freezer without getting icy. My solution: just a little cranberry juice concentrate instead. (Meanwhile, plenty of other drinks, like the Negroni and Old Fashioned, enter the bottle in their classic forms just fine.)

Other tricks include using the blender to create speed infusions, an easy way to deliver tons of flavor to a liquor without adding juice or water (thereby keeping it freezer-friendly), and fat-washing, a simple but delicious way to flavor a cocktail with something fatty, such as bacon or coconut milk, without actually adding anything to the drink.

Some cocktails also are served differently. When traditional cocktails are mixed, most of them are shaken or stirred with ice. This not only chills cocktails, it also dilutes them. To compensate, I often add some water to the bottle. But some recipes need more dilution than others, and above a certain threshold, that water can freeze. In these cases, I suggest serving the drink over ice, even if the cocktail isn't traditionally served on ice.

My goal is to make it easy for everyone to keep bottles of their go-to cocktails on standby, whether for a party or a party of one. Consider it inspiration to finally eat all those frozen leftovers and lonely bags of peas, and put your freezer space to better use.

Finally, like my books *Shake Strain Done: Craft Cocktails at Home* and *Pour Me Another: 250 Ways to Find Your Favorite Drink*, the recipes in this book are written in a language you can taste. Each cocktail is described with a spectrum of terms that we understand—and can "taste"—long before our lips ever touch the glass. Every cocktail is identified by some combination of characteristics—**REFRESHING, CREAMY, FRUITY, SWEET, SOUR, HERBAL, BITTER, SPICY, SMOKY, WARM** and **STRONG**—and they are ordered from most to least dominant. This not only communicates what's in the glass, it also helps identify relationships between cocktails that may seem quite different on the surface but in fact offer similar constellations of flavors.

FREEZER COCKTAILS

THE SCIENCE OF FREEZER COCKTAILS

You don't need to understand the science behind these cocktails to make and enjoy them, so if you'd rather skip to the mixing and drinking, by all means, flip to page 9. But if you'd like to experiment with your own recipes—or if your freezer gives you trouble with the ones in this book—it helps to understand what is happening in the bottle.

You may be familiar with the convention of storing vodka in the freezer. It works because the typical home freezer is set between 0°F and -15°F (-18°C and -26°C), which is plenty cold enough to keep your vegetables and ice frozen. But alcohol has a much lower freezing point. The closer a beverage is to being 100 percent alcohol, the lower the temperature must be for it to freeze.

Liquor that is 40 percent alcohol by volume (ABV)—which accounts for most base liquors, including whiskey, vodka, tequila, gin and rum—freezes at -16.5°F (-27°C). By comparison, wine, which ranges from 12 to 15 percent ABV, freezes at a relatively balmy 20°F (-6.5°C); and beer, which generally has an ABV of 4 to 7 percent, can freeze around 28°F (-2°C).

This means that any bottle of 40 percent ABV liquor can be stored in the average home freezer without worry. But adding cocktail ingredients, such as juices, syrups or even lower-ABV liqueurs, changes the volume of alcohol in the bottle, and that changes the freezing point of the mixture.

For example, a cocktail made from half gin and half other ingredients (such as tonic water and juice) drops from 40 percent ABV to 20 percent ABV, which can freeze at around 19°F (-7°C). In most home freezers, that cocktail will become an ice cube.

For this reason, a freezer cocktail should never contain more than 20 percent no- or low-ABV ingredients, such as water or juice. That means you could replace a fifth of a full bottle of 40 percent ABV liquor with no- or low-ABV ingredients, and it will freeze only if kept at -10°F (-23.5°C) or colder. This is why freezer cocktails don't always use the same ratios as conventional cocktails.

WHAT ABOUT THE WATER?

When most cocktails are made, they are either shaken or stirred with ice, regardless of whether they will be served on ice. This chills and dilutes them. That dilution is important: a little water opens up the flavors of the liquor, making them easier to taste and appreciate.

Accounting for this often is a matter of adding a little water to the bottle. But it's not always so simple. If a cocktail already is maxed out with other no- and low-ABV ingredients, adding water can make it susceptible to freezing.

To keep those cocktails freezer-friendly, some are served on ice, even if they traditionally would not be (as in my freezer Manhattan, page 138). That allows for the necessary dilution. Alternatively, you can simply stir 1 to 2 teaspoons of water into the serving glass, then taste and adjust.

MY COCKTAIL FROZE!

If you have trouble with your cocktails freezing, your freezer itself likely is the culprit. Though manufacturers say they set home freezers to about 0°F (-18°C), many actually operate much colder than that. To identify the problem, purchase a freezer thermometer (available cheaply online and at hardware stores). Fancy models even let you monitor the temperature from a smartphone. Don't trust thermometers built into the freezer; they rarely are accurate.

If you find your freezer is running too cold, adjust it a little at a time, giving the freezer about 12 to 24 hours between each adjustment, until it maintains a temperature closer to 0°F (-18°C).

If your cocktail does freeze, leaving it at room temperature for a few minutes will return it to liquid form. Likewise, if your cocktail turns slushy but doesn't freeze solid, give the bottle a few good shakes and it will be perfectly pourable.

TAKE A BEAT?

The trouble with cold is that it dulls flavor. This is why even ice cream tastes better if you let it warm a bit before eating. The same is true for all cocktails, not only those stored in the freezer. In fact, I often will remove the ice from my cocktail after a few minutes, which prevents it from overchilling or overdiluting the drink.

With freezer cocktails, the drink itself already has been chilled, likely to at least 0°F (-18°C). But most traditional cocktails that have been shaken or stirred with ice are served at around 20°F (-6.5°C). So it's not a bad thing to give your freezer cocktail a brief rest in the glass to warm up. A few minutes will suffice.

CAN I SKIP THE FREEZER?

If you'd prefer to store your bottled cocktails in the refrigerator or at room temperature, you have options. Cocktails made entirely from liquor-based ingredients can be stored indefinitely in the refrigerator or at room temperature. Anything with citrus juice or other ingredients that may spoil can be refrigerated for up to a week; they should not be stored at room temperature for more than a few hours.

FAT-WASHING

The freezer isn't just a great place to store batched cocktails. When you use a technique called fat-washing, it's also a great way to flavor them. Fat-washing infuses liquor with the flavor of a fatty ingredient, such as bacon or coconut oil, without adding the actual ingredient to the drink.

It works because fatty ingredients contain plenty of alcohol-soluble flavor molecules. When you combine a flavorful fat and a liquor, those molecules infuse the liquor. A few minutes of steeping is all it takes. After that, you pop the liquor in the freezer, which causes the fat to freeze on the surface. It's then easy to strain out the fat, leaving nothing but its flavor behind.

FINISHED WITH A SPLASH

Some cocktails need a finishing splash of something that can't go in the freezer, such as soda water or sparkling wine. Or sometimes a cocktail—think a Bloody Mary—is finished with so much juice that the cocktail would freeze if the juice was added to the bottle. A few recipes call for adding this sort of finishing splash only at the time of serving.

ESSENTIAL GEAR

One of the joys of freezer cocktails is that almost no special equipment is needed. Because the drinks are built directly in a bottle, not even a cocktail shaker is used. But there are some simple and inexpensive tools that will make crafting these cocktails easier.

BOTTLES

Kind of obvious. Each of these recipes makes a full bottle of cocktail, which is 750 milliliters, or about $25^{1/3}$ ounces. So for each recipe, you will need one standard-size liquor bottle. By the way, you might notice—or even get annoyed—that I offer both imperial and metric measurements throughout the book. This is to make your life easier. Most liquor bottles are labeled in milliliters, but you may be more comfortable using imperial (ounces, teaspoons, etc.) when measuring ingredients.

If you plan to make freezer cocktails by pouring off some of a full bottle of the drink's primary liquor, the bottle takes care of itself. Buy a 750-milliliter bottle of that liquor, and you are set. But if you prefer to combine everything in a fresh bottle, you have plenty of options.

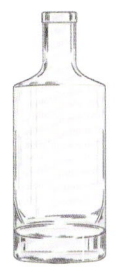

Obviously, rather than adding your empty liquor bottles to the recycling bin, you can simply wash out one, remove the label (if you care), and build your cocktail in that. Another option is large preserving jars, which can accommodate 946 milliliters, so you'll have a little extra space. They also are easy to fill.

If you want your freezer to get classy, check out Crew Supply Co.'s Crew Bottle in the USA, a rugged, long-necked 850-milliliter bottle with a removable base. In addition to looking sexy, their bottles are designed to handle extreme temperatures, while the removable bottoms allow the bottles to go in the dishwasher.

BLENDER

Many cocktails call for juice, but adding too much will cause these cocktails to freeze. So if a recipe needs more citrus flavor than we can get from a couple of ounces, we use the blender to create speed infusions. This involves using a vegetable peeler to strip the flavorful zest from citrus fruit, then combining it with a liquor in the blender. A few pulses—just enough to chop the zest but not puree it—is all it takes to infuse the liquor with bold citrus flavor.

Astute readers might notice that some blender infusion recipes require ingredients with a combined total volume that exceeds the capacity of a 750-milliliter bottle. Relax. The straining process causes a small amount of liquor loss. Those recipes build in extra liquor to compensate for that.

MESH SIEVE AND MUSLIN

Recipes that involve blender speed infusions or fat-washing need to be strained before bottling. A mesh sieve lined with muslin works best.

FUNNEL

Unless you plan to prepare your cocktails only in preserving jars, which have a wide mouth that makes filling them simple, you will want a funnel. This makes it faster and easier to add the cocktail ingredients to liquor bottles.

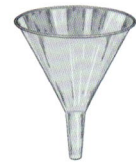

ICE

Because these recipes are not shaken or stirred in the conventional way, ice is used only for serving. For standard ice cubes, use whatever variety you have. But many cocktail enthusiasts prefer to use oversize ice cubes; they chill better and melt more slowly

than standard ice cubes. Silicone molds for making large ice cubes are cheap and widely available. For crushed ice, a cloth Lewis bag and wooden mallet are great, but a heavy-duty plastic bag and a rolling pin work well, too.

JIGGERS AND MEASURING CUPS

For measuring cocktail ingredients, it's good to have a 2-cup (16-oz/500-ml) liquid measuring cup, as well as a smaller 2-ounce (60-ml) jigger. I prefer the OXO 2-Cup Angled Measuring Cup and the OXO Steel Angled Jigger.

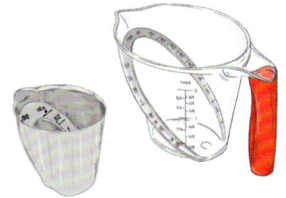

FREEZER THERMOMETER

A freezer thermometer is needed only if you are having trouble with your cocktails freezing. This means your freezer is set below 0°F (-18°C). The easiest way to check it is to use an inexpensive freezer thermometer. Most are simply placed inside the freezer (hanging from a shelf is ideal). Fancier models can mount on the outside of the door or even send updates to your phone.

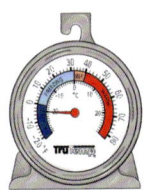

Y-STYLE VEGETABLE PEELER

A very sharp, lightweight vegetable peeler is the best tool for removing thin strips of citrus zest, which are used throughout this book both for garnishes and to flavor liquors.

ESSENTIAL GEAR

VODKA

Bitter Blood Martini BITTER | SWEET | STRONG

The combination of orange-infused vodka and bittersweet Campari creates a simple and stunning cocktail. If you prefer less bitterness, substitute Aperol for the Campari. I also add a bit of vanilla-spiced Licor 43 because the sweetness tames the vodka and Campari and delivers smooth, creamy notes.

 STARTING WITH A FULL BOTTLE?
Pour off 10 ounces (300 ml).

MAKES 5 TO 7 COCKTAILS

15 ounces (450 ml) vodka

Zest strips from 1 large orange

5¼ ounces (158 ml) Campari

3 ounces (90 ml) water

1¾ ounces (53 ml) Licor 43

1 ounce (30 ml) agave or simple syrup

Crushed ice, to serve

In a blender, combine the vodka and orange zest. Pulse until finely chopped but not pureed. Let sit for 3 minutes. Strain the vodka through a muslin-lined mesh sieve into a 750-milliliter bottle. Add the Campari, water, Licor 43 and syrup. Cap the bottle securely, then shake well to mix. Store in the freezer. To serve, pour into a cocktail glass filled halfway with crushed ice.

Thirsty for more?
If you have some vodka to spare, try a:

Mr. 404 FRUITY | SWEET | BITTER | REFRESHING

MAKES 1 COCKTAIL

1½ ounces (45 ml) vodka

½ ounce (15 ml) elderflower liqueur

½ ounce (15 ml) Aperol

¼ ounce (8 ml) lemon juice

¾ teaspoon (4 ml) agave or simple syrup

Ice cubes

Orange zest twist

In a cocktail shaker, combine the vodka, elderflower liqueur, Aperol, lemon juice and syrup. Shake with ice cubes, then strain into a cocktail glass. Garnish with the orange twist.

Black (and White) Russian CREAMY | SWEET | STRONG

The Black Russian is not as well-known as its cousin, the White Russian, but it deserves some attention. Especially in the freezer. Though the cocktail requires just vodka and Kahlúa, the latter liquor packs a three-stroke flavor punch in one ingredient—rum, sweetener and coffee. The resulting cocktail is rich, creamy and lightly sweet. Want to transform this into the signature White Russian of the movie *The Big Lebowski*? Serve the Black Russian as directed, then top it with a splash of double cream.

STARTING WITH A FULL BOTTLE?
Pour off 9 ounces (270 ml).
MAKES 5 TO 7 COCKTAILS

16 ounces (480 ml) vodka

8 ounces (240 ml) Kahlúa

Ice cubes, to serve

In a 750-milliliter bottle, combine the vodka and Kahlúa. Cap the bottle securely, then shake well to mix. Store in the freezer. To serve, pour into a rocks glass with 1 large or 3 standard ice cubes.

Thirsty for more?
If you have some vodka to spare, try a:

White(-ish) Russian CREAMY | SWEET | STRONG

MAKES 1 COCKTAIL

2 ounces (60 ml) vodka

1½ ounces (45 ml) coconut water

1 ounce (30 ml) Kahlúa

6 to 10 granules sea salt

Ice cubes

In a cocktail shaker, combine the vodka, coconut water, Kahlúa and salt. Shake with ice cubes, then strain into a Nick and Nora glass.

Bloody Mary   REFRESHING | SPICY | SWEET

I don't like adapting cocktails to the freezer if doing so requires leaving out a key ingredient. The whole point is one-bottle ease! But the Bloody Mary is too iconic—and, let's be honest, too important to our emotional well-being—to ignore. So I give you the perfect Bloody Mary mixer. Prep this bottle as directed, then serve by adding it to a highball glass of ice and tomato or vegetable juice. (I prefer the latter, but you do you.) And, of course, garnish as you see fit! I keep it simple with celery and (when I'm feeling fancy) bacon. But if you feel the need to top Mary with a full hamburger, go for it.

 STARTING WITH A FULL BOTTLE?
Pour off 5 ounces (150 ml).

MAKES 6 COCKTAILS

- 20 ounces (600 ml) vodka
- 2 ounces (60 ml) lemon juice
- 1 ounce (30 ml) agave or simple syrup
- 1 teaspoon (5 ml) soy sauce
- 1 teaspoon (5 ml) Worcestershire sauce
- ½ teaspoon (3 ml) Tabasco (or more, to taste), plus more to serve
- Pinch celery salt
- Pinch smoked paprika
- Ice cubes, to serve
- Tomato or vegetable juice, to serve

In a 750-milliliter bottle, combine the vodka, lemon juice, syrup, soy sauce, Worcestershire sauce, Tabasco, celery salt and smoked paprika. Cap the bottle securely, then shake well to mix. Store in the freezer. To serve, shake well and pour 4 ounces (120 ml) into a generous highball glass filled halfway with ice cubes. Top with 3 to 4 ounces (90 to 120 ml) tomato or vegetable juice. Stir, then garnish as desired.

Thirsty for more?
If you have some vodka to spare, try a:

Rio Jengibre REFRESHING | SPICY | SOUR

MAKES 1 COCKTAIL
- Orange zest strip
- 2 coins fresh ginger
- ½ ounce (15 ml) agave or simple syrup
- ¼ ounce (8 ml) lime juice
- 3 ounces (90 ml) vodka
- Ice, cubes and crushed

In a cocktail shaker, muddle the zest strip, ginger, syrup and lime juice. Add the vodka. Shake with ice cubes, then double strain into a coupe filled halfway with crushed ice.

Brando Russian   CREAMY | STRONG | SWEET

What do you get when you cross an ice lolly with a Black Russian? The Brando Russian, a creamy, citrusy and rich cocktail that goes down way too easy. The Black Russian supposedly was created during the late 1940s in Belgium by barman Gustave Tops. It is a basic blend of two parts vodka to one part Kahlúa (see page 12). Add double cream or milk, and it becomes a White Russian. Or skip the dairy and add orange liqueur and orange bitters, and you get a Brando Russian. Want to make it a White Brando Russian? Serve as directed and top the glass with a splash of double cream.

 STARTING WITH A FULL BOTTLE?
Pour off 11 ounces (330 ml).
MAKES 5 TO 7 COCKTAILS

14 ounces (420 ml) vodka

7 ounces (210 ml) Kahlúa

1¾ ounces (53 ml) orange liqueur

¼ teaspoon (2 ml) orange bitters

Ice cubes, to serve

In a 750-milliliter bottle, combine the vodka, Kahlúa, orange liqueur and bitters. Cap the bottle securely, then shake well to mix. Store in the freezer. To serve, pour into a rocks glass with 1 large or 3 standard ice cubes.

Thirsty for more?
If you have some vodka to spare, try a:

Chai Slide   CREAMY | STRONG | SWEET | SPICY

MAKES 1 COCKTAIL

1 bag chai tea

2 ounces (60 ml) boiling water

3 ounces (90 ml) vodka

1 ounce (30 ml) whole milk

½ ounce (15 ml) agave or simple syrup

Generous pinch unsweetened cocoa powder, plus extra to garnish

Ice cubes

In a cup, combine the tea bag and boiling water. Steep for 2 minutes. Squeeze the tea bag into the cup, then discard. In a cocktail shaker, combine the tea, vodka, milk, syrup and cocoa powder. Shake with ice cubes. Strain into a rocks glass. Lightly dust with cocoa powder.

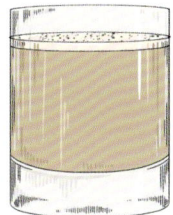

Caribbean Cruise STRONG | CREAMY | SWEET

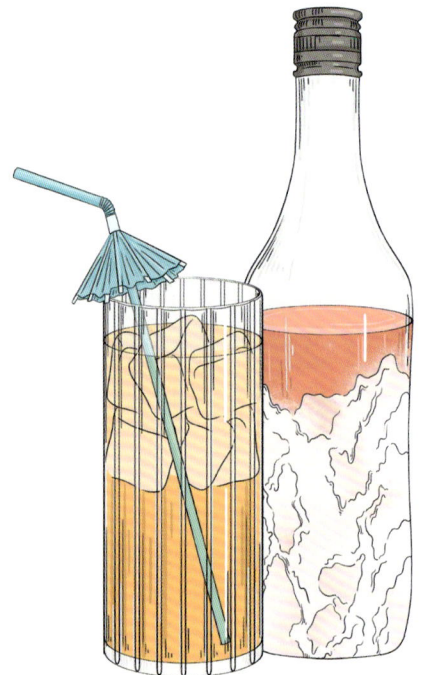

To maximize the summer vibes of this tiki-style cocktail, make sure you get a fancy straw and stake out a good spot at the pool or beach. Pack a cooler with ice, and all you need is a bit of pineapple juice to tie it all together.

 STARTING WITH A FULL BOTTLE?
Pour off 12 ounces (360 ml).

MAKES 8 COCKTAILS

13 ounces (390 ml) vodka

6½ ounces (195 ml) white rum

3½ ounces (105 ml) coconut rum

1 ounce (30 ml) grenadine

Ice cubes, to serve

Pineapple juice, to serve

In a 750-milliliter bottle, combine the vodka, white rum, coconut rum and grenadine. Cap the bottle securely, then shake well to mix. Store in the freezer. To serve, pour about 3 ounces (90 ml) into a highball glass filled halfway with ice cubes. Top with 2 to 4 ounces (60 to 120 ml) pineapple juice. Stir with a straw.

Thirsty for more?
If you have some white rum to spare, try a:

Fog Cutter REFRESHING | SWEET

MAKES 1 COCKTAIL

2 ounces (60 ml) white rum

1 ounce (30 ml) aged rum

1 ounce (30 ml) pulp-free orange juice

½ ounce (15 ml) orgeat syrup (an almond sugar syrup)

½ ounce (15 ml) gin

½ ounce (15 ml) Cognac

½ ounce (15 ml) dry sherry

½ ounce (15 ml) pisco

¼ ounce (8 ml) agave or simple syrup

¼ ounce (8 ml) pineapple juice

Dash Angostura bitters

6 to 10 granules sea salt

Ice cubes

1 sprig fresh mint

1 maraschino cherry

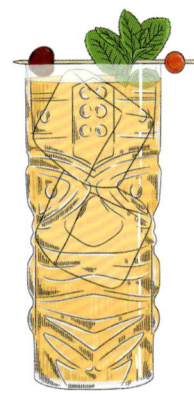

In a cocktail shaker, combine the white rum, aged rum, orange juice, orgeat syrup, gin, Cognac, dry sherry, pisco, syrup, pineapple juice, bitters and salt. Shake with ice cubes, then strain into a highball glass with 2 large or 4 to 6 standard ice cubes. Top with the mint and cherry.

Cosmopolitan SWEET | SOUR | REFRESHING | STRONG

This tart and sweet sipper belongs at-the-ready in everyone's home. Especially for those nights when you need to feel a little sexy. Adapting the classic Cosmo—a blend of citrus-flavored vodka, orange liqueur, lime juice, sugar and cranberry juice—for the freezer took a bit of tweaking. But it was worth it. The traditional proportions tend to turn slushy in the freezer. The culprit was the cranberry juice. The simple solution was cranberry juice concentrate, which has tons of flavor and little water. Just 1 ounce (30 ml) was plenty to give this cocktail all the flavor needed. Cranberry juice concentrate is available at most health food shops and online. Combined with the orange liqueur and orange bitters, ¼ ounce (8 ml) lime juice is more than enough to give the cocktail its trademark tang.

 STARTING WITH A FULL BOTTLE?
Pour off 9 ounces (270 ml).

MAKES 5 TO 7 COCKTAILS

- 16 ounces (480 ml) vodka
- 3 ounces (90 ml) orange liqueur
- 2 ounces (60 ml) water
- 1½ ounces (45 ml) agave or simple syrup
- 1 ounce (30 ml) cranberry juice concentrate
- ¼ ounce (8 ml) lime juice
- ¼ teaspoon (2 ml) orange bitters
- Ice cubes, to serve

In a 750-milliliter bottle, combine the vodka, orange liqueur, water, syrup, cranberry juice concentrate, lime juice and bitters. Cap the bottle securely, then shake well to mix. Store in the freezer. To serve, pour into a cocktail glass with 1 standard ice cube.

Thirsty for more?
If you have some vodka to spare, try a:

Bay Breeze REFRESHING | FRUITY

MAKES 1 COCKTAIL

- 3 ounces (90 ml) vodka
- 3 ounces (90 ml) sweetened cranberry juice
- 3 ounces (90 ml) pineapple juice
- Dash Angostura bitters
- 6 to 10 granules sea salt
- Ice cubes
- 1 lime wedge

In a cocktail shaker, combine the vodka, cranberry juice, pineapple juice, bitters and salt. Shake with ice cubes, then strain into a highball glass filled halfway with ice. Squeeze the lime wedge over the drink, then add it to the glass.

Espresso Martini   STRONG | CREAMY | SWEET | BITTER

This one is for when you want to raid the freezer at midnight! Creating a freezer version of Dick Bradsell's classic Espresso Martini required a fair bit of tinkering. Using freshly brewed espresso—as is traditional—wasn't an option. Adding enough espresso for the finished cocktail to taste rich and bold added too much water, which froze. The solution was instant espresso powder, which adds tons of flavor and no water. It also gives the cocktail a pleasant viscosity that mirrors the frothiness you get from shaking. To account for the dilution that occurs during shaking with ice, a bit of water is needed, but not nearly as much as with freshly brewed espresso. Be sure to use instant espresso powder, often sold near the baking ingredients, not ground espresso, which won't dissolve.

STARTING WITH A FULL BOTTLE?
Pour off 10 ounces (300 ml).
MAKES 5 TO 7 COCKTAILS

15 ounces (450 ml) vodka

9 ounces (270 ml) Kahlúa

3½ tablespoons (20 g) instant espresso powder

1 ounce (30 ml) water

Ice cubes, to serve

In a 750-milliliter bottle, combine the vodka, Kahlúa, espresso powder and water. Cap the bottle securely, then shake very well to mix. Store in the freezer. To serve, pour into a rocks glass with 1 large ice cube.

Thirsty for more?
If you have some vodka to spare, try a:

Coffee Cargo Cocktail STRONG | CREAMY

MAKES 1 COCKTAIL

1 scoop vanilla ice cream

2 ounces (60 ml) vodka

1 ounce (30 ml) Kahlúa

2 ounces (60 ml) espresso, cooled

In a stirring glass, combine the ice cream, vodka, Kahlúa and espresso. Stir for 1 minute, or until the ice cream has melted. Pour into a coupe.

French Martini   FRUITY | STRONG | REFRESHING

The freezer is the true friend of the flavored Martinis. So many of them work so perfectly, as they absolutely love subzero temperatures. No exception is the cocktail most bartending folks credit with starting the flavored martini trend back in the 1980s—the French Martini. The combination of vodka, Chambord (a French raspberry liqueur) and pineapple juice—introduced in New York City by Keith McNally—drinks easily without being cloyingly sweet. Adapting it to the freezer produced a more nuanced version of the classic. I dialed back the pineapple juice, which often is added at near equal proportions to the vodka. That ratio blots out the fruity sweetness of the Chambord. It's worth noting that some people make this with gin instead of vodka. If you're looking for a more botanical cocktail, go for it.

 **STARTING WITH A FULL BOTTLE?**
Pour off 10½ ounces (315 ml).
MAKES 5 TO 7 COCKTAILS

14½ ounces (435 ml) vodka
5¼ ounces (158 ml) Chambord
3 ounces (90 ml) water
1¾ ounces (53 ml) pineapple juice
Lemon zest strips, to serve

In a 750-milliliter bottle, combine the vodka, Chambord, water and pineapple juice. Cap the bottle securely, then shake well to mix. Store in the freezer. To serve, rub a lemon zest strip around the rim of a cocktail glass, then add it to the glass. Pour the cocktail into the glass.

Thirsty for more?
If you have some vodka to spare, try an:

All Jammed Up SWEET | FRUITY | SPICY

MAKES 1 COCKTAIL

2½ ounces (75 ml) vodka
¼ ounce (8 ml) orange liqueur
¼ ounce (8 ml) Ancho Reyes chili liqueur
1 teaspoon raspberry jam
Ice cubes

In a cocktail shaker, combine the vodka, orange liqueur, Ancho Reyes and jam. Shake with ice cubes, then double strain into a cocktail glass with 1 large or 2 standard ice cubes.

Gingersnap Martini FRUITY | SWEET | STRONG

Sweet, sassy and snappy. That's the Gingersnap Martini. It's a riff on the French Martini that uses ginger and orange liqueurs to create a brighter, less fruity cocktail with more peppery zip. If you want a dirty Gingersnap Martini, add a splash of green olive brine to each glass, or just add a skewered green olive to each glass for stirring. Or lean into the gingersnap vibe and offer cookies for dunking.

STARTING WITH A FULL BOTTLE?
Pour off 7½ ounces (225 ml).

MAKES 5 TO 7 COCKTAILS

17½ ounces (525 ml) vodka
3 ounces (90 ml) water
3 ounces (90 ml) ginger liqueur
1 ounce (30 ml) orange liqueur
1 tablespoon (12 g) white sugar, to serve
½ teaspoon (3 g) ground ginger, to serve
Water or lemon juice, to serve

In a 750-milliliter bottle, combine the vodka, water, ginger liqueur and orange liqueur. Cap the bottle securely, then shake well to mix. Store in the freezer. To serve, on a small plate stir together the sugar and ginger. Wet the rim of a cocktail glass with water or lemon juice, then overturn the glass into the sugar-ginger mixture, gently moving the glass to coat the rim. Right the glass and pour the cocktail into it.

Thirsty for more?
If you have some vodka to spare, try a:

Bitter Bastard STRONG | FRUITY | BITTER | SWEET

MAKES 1 COCKTAIL

2 ounces (60 ml) vodka
1 ounce (30 ml) Aperol
1 ounce (30 ml) grapefruit juice
Dash orange bitters
6 to 10 granules sea salt
Ice cubes
Sparkling wine

In a cocktail shaker, combine the vodka, Aperol, grapefruit juice, bitters and salt. Shake with ice cubes. Strain into a coupe. Top with sparkling wine.

(High-End) Harvey Wallbanger   FRUITY | HERBAL | SWEET

The original Harvey Wallbanger, which dates to the 1950s, is basically a Screwdriver (vodka and orange juice) adulterated with Galliano, an Italian liqueur with sweet, herbal and vanilla notes. Adapting it for the freezer was an opportunity to make this Mimosa-type cocktail a little upmarket. I like to batch the main ingredients and store them in the freezer. When it's time to serve, I pour it into a cocktail glass or coupe (rather than the more traditional highball) and top it with a splash of sparkling wine. The result is lightly sweet, a little fruity and deliciously effervescent.

STARTING WITH A FULL BOTTLE?
Pour off 8 ounces (240 ml).

MAKES 5 TO 7 COCKTAILS

17 ounces (510 ml) vodka

5 ounces (150 ml) Galliano

2 ounces (60 ml) pulp-free orange juice

Sparkling wine, to serve

In a 750-milliliter bottle, combine the vodka, Galliano and orange juice. Cap the bottle securely, then shake well to mix. Store in the freezer. To serve, shake the bottle, then pour into a cocktail glass and top with 1 to 2 ounces (30 to 60 ml) of sparkling wine.

Thirsty for more?
If you have some vodka to spare, try a:

Moscow's Sunny Side CREAMY | FRUITY | SWEET

MAKES 1 COCKTAIL

3 ounces (90 ml) vodka

¼ vanilla bean, cut into pieces

Half orange slice with skin

¼ ounce (8 ml) agave or simple syrup

Ice, cubes and crushed

Orange zest twist

In a blender, combine the vodka, vanilla bean, orange slice and syrup. Blend for 5 seconds or until the bean is well chopped but not pureed. Strain through a mesh cocktail sieve lined with a muslin into a cocktail shaker. Shake with ice cubes. Double strain into a coupe filled halfway with crushed ice. Garnish with the orange zest twist.

VODKA 29

Lemon Drop SOUR | SWEET | FRUITY

The classic Lemon Drop is a sweet-and-sour crowd-pleaser perfect for a freezer overhaul. Many people credit the original recipe to Norman Jay Hobday, a San Francisco bar owner from the 1970s, but it likely is based on the Crusta, a drink that dates back more than 100 years before that. Traditionally, it's vodka, equal parts lemon juice and sugar, plus a bit of orange liqueur. Here, we tamp down the lemon juice and sugar, both of which can make the cocktail susceptible to freezing. To compensate, we add a few ounces of limoncello, a sweet-and-sour Italian liqueur.

 STARTING WITH A FULL BOTTLE?
Pour off 13 ounces (390 ml).
MAKES 5 TO 7 COCKTAILS

- 12 ounces (360 ml) vodka
- 4½ ounces (135 ml) orange liqueur
- 3 ounces (90 ml) limoncello
- 1½ ounces (45 ml) lemon juice
- 1½ ounces (45 ml) water
- 1½ ounces (45 ml) agave or simple syrup
- Lemon zest strips, to serve

In a 750-milliliter bottle, combine the vodka, orange liqueur, limoncello, lemon juice, water and syrup. Cap the bottle securely, then shake to mix. Store in the freezer. To serve, pour into a cocktail glass and add a lemon zest strip.

Thirsty for more?
If you have some vodka to spare, try a:

Vodka Special SWEET | SOUR | STRONG | FRUITY

MAKES 1 COCKTAIL
- 2 ounces (60 ml) vodka
- ½ ounce (15 ml) maraschino liqueur
- ¼ ounce (8 ml) lime juice
- ¼ ounce (8 ml) agave or simple syrup
- 6 to 10 granules sea salt
- Ice cubes

In a cocktail shaker, combine the vodka, maraschino liqueur, lime juice, syrup and salt. Shake with ice cubes, then strain into a cocktail glass.

Long Island Iced Tea SWEET | STRONG

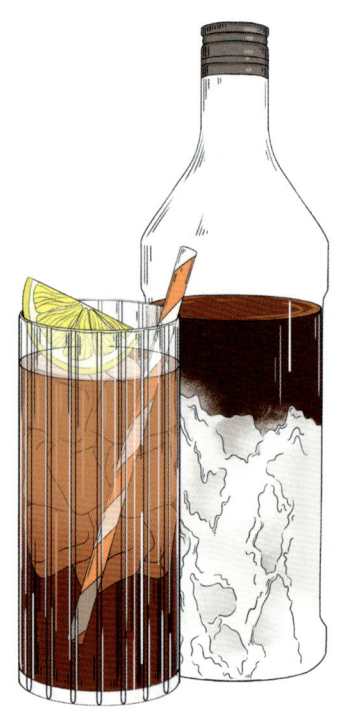

The Long Island Iced Tea really is the trash can of cocktails. Deliciously so. That said, it is possible to craft a balanced version that tastes great and allows the individual ingredients to shine. The classic Long Island Iced Tea is a blend of five liquors—vodka, tequila, gin, rum and orange liqueur—all topped with a healthy splash of cola. Since carbonated drinks can't be frozen, for the freezer version we use cola syrup instead (the type used to flavor carbonated water). When served, the cocktail is finished with a dash of carbonated water. The syrup is sold alongside water flavorings at most supermarkets. If you'd prefer to use regular cola, simply skip the syrup; to serve, replace the carbonated water with an equal amount of cola. Unlike most freezer recipes, which begin by pouring off a bit of liquor from the cocktail's primary ingredient, there are so many ingredients in this one, it's easier to build it in an empty bottle.

MAKES 5 TO 7 COCKTAILS

- 7 ounces (210 ml) vodka
- 3½ ounces (105 ml) blanco tequila
- 3½ ounces (105 ml) gin
- 3½ ounces (105 ml) white rum
- 1¾ ounces (53 ml) orange liqueur
- 1¾ ounces (53 ml) lemon juice
- 1¾ ounces (53 ml) cola syrup
- Ice cubes, to serve
- Carbonated water, to serve
- Lemon wedges, to serve

In a 750-milliliter bottle, combine the vodka, tequila, gin, rum, orange liqueur, lemon juice and cola syrup. Cap the bottle securely, then shake well to mix. Store in the freezer. To serve, fill a highball glass two-thirds with ice cubes, then add an equal amount of the cocktail. Top with about 2 ounces (60 ml) carbonated water. Garnish with a lemon wedge.

Thirsty for more?
If you have some vodka to spare, try a:

Ginger Screw   FRUITY | SWEET | STRONG

MAKES 1 COCKTAIL
- 2 ounces (60 ml) vodka
- 1 ounce (30 ml) pulp-free orange juice
- ½ ounce (15 ml) ginger liqueur
- 6 to 10 granules sea salt
- Ice cubes

In a cocktail shaker, combine the vodka, orange juice, ginger liqueur and salt. Shake with ice cubes, then strain into a cocktail glass.

Moscow Mule STRONG | SPICY | SOUR

The classic Moscow Mule is a potent blend of vodka, lime juice and ginger beer. The trouble is the potency. The lime juice and ginger beer are a bold combination. I'd argue too bold. Mind you, I don't want to lose those flavors; I just want to tame them so they are a bit more balanced, and less sugary and acidic. My solution—a speed infusion that brings this cocktail back to its flavor roots and makes it friendly for the freezer. We use the blender to combine vodka, fresh ginger and lime zest, pulse it briefly, then let it infuse for a few minutes. Strain out the solids and you have ginger-lime vodka, the perfect base for a deliciously balanced Moscow Mule.

 STARTING WITH A FULL BOTTLE?
Pour off 6 ounces (180 ml).
MAKES 8 COCKTAILS

19 ounces (570 ml) vodka

1-inch (2-cm) chunk fresh ginger, cut into 4 pieces

2 ounces (60 ml) agave or simple syrup

Zest strips from 1 lime

Pinch sea salt

2 ounces (60 ml) ginger liqueur

1 ounce (30 ml) lime juice

Ice cubes, to serve

Carbonated water, to serve

Lime rounds, to serve

In a blender, combine the vodka, ginger, syrup, lime zest strips and salt. Pulse until the zest and ginger are finely chopped but not pureed. Let sit for 3 minutes. Strain through a muslin-lined mesh sieve into a 750-milliliter bottle. Add the ginger liqueur and lime juice. Cap the bottle securely, shake, then store in the freezer. To serve, pour 3 ounces (90 ml) into an ice-filled highball glass, then top with a splash of carbonated water. Stir gently, then garnish with a lime round.

Thirsty for more?
If you have some vodka to spare, try a:

Mint Fizz STRONG | HERBAL | REFRESHING | SOUR

MAKES 1 COCKTAIL

2 sprigs fresh mint

½ ounce (15 ml) orgeat syrup (simple or agave syrup can be substituted)

3 ounces (90 ml) vodka

¼ ounce (8 ml) lemon juice

Ice, cubes and crushed

1 ounce (30 ml) club soda

In a cocktail shaker, muddle the mint and orgeat syrup. Leave the muddler in the shaker. Add the vodka and lemon juice, then swish the muddler to rinse. Remove the muddler. Shake with ice cubes. Strain into a coupe filled halfway with crushed ice. Top with club soda.

VODKA

Tahini Martini STRONG | SWEET | BITTER

The Tahini Martini shows off the savory side of cocktails. Tahini, a rich paste made from ground sesame seeds, has a creamy, savory flavor that loves lemon. And vodka! This recipe requires multiple steps, but none is difficult. You will need two squares of muslin, as the vodka is infused twice—first with lemon zest in the blender, then with tahini in the freezer. In both cases, the solids need to be strained out and discarded.

 STARTING WITH A FULL BOTTLE?
Pour off 4 ounces (120 ml).

MAKES 5 TO 7 COCKTAILS

21 ounces (630 ml) vodka

Zest strips from 1 lemon

2 tablespoons (30 ml) tahini

2 ounces (60 ml) water

1¾ ounces (53 ml) agave or simple syrup

¼ teaspoon (2 ml) orange bitters

Fresh mint leaves, to serve

In a blender, combine the vodka and lemon zest. Pulse until finely chopped but not pureed. Let sit for 3 minutes. Strain through a muslin-lined mesh sieve into a liquid measuring cup with at least a 4-cup (2-pint or 1-liter) capacity. Discard the zest. Stir the tahini into the vodka; it won't be smooth. Let sit at room temperature for 5 minutes, stirring often. Place in the freezer for 30 minutes. Strain again through a mesh sieve lined with a fresh piece of muslin into a 750-milliliter bottle; discard the solids. Add the water, syrup and bitters. Cap the bottle securely, then shake well to mix. Store in the freezer. To serve, shake the bottle (some sediment on the bottom is normal), and pour into a cocktail glass. Garnish with a mint leaf.

Thirsty for more?
If you have some vodka to spare, try a:

Little Miss Sunshine STRONG | SWEET | BITTER | REFRESHING

MAKES 1 COCKTAIL

2 ounces (60 ml) vodka

2 saffron threads

1 ounce (30 ml) dry vermouth

¼ ounce (8 ml) agave or simple syrup

6 to 10 granules sea salt

Ice, cubes and crushed

Add the vodka to a cocktail shaker. Use your fingers to crush the saffron into it. Swirl and let steep for 5 minutes. Add the vermouth, syrup and salt. Shake with ice cubes. Strain into a cocktail glass filled halfway with crushed ice.

VODKA 37

Vodka Martini STRONG

If you're a gin purist when it comes to the Martini, head to page 78. But for those of us who enjoy the clean, crisp flavor clarity of the vodka version, here is your answer to having the perfect cocktail on tap and at the ready. Don't skip the water in this recipe. It's important to account for the dilution that would occur if you were stirring (or, god help you, shaking) the cocktail with ice. If you prefer your Martini clean, skip the olive brine. Just replace it with an additional 1¼ ounces (38 ml) of vodka and ¼ ounce (8 ml) of water. For serving, be sure to have high-quality green olives on hand. I prefer Castelvetrano (also known as Nocellara), which are meaty and briny.

 **STARTING WITH A FULL BOTTLE?**
Pour off 8 ounces (240 ml).
MAKES 5 TO 7 COCKTAILS

17 ounces (510 ml) vodka

4 ounces (120 ml) dry vermouth

2½ ounces (75 ml) water

1½ ounces (45 ml) green olive brine (optional)

Green olives, to serve

In a 750-milliliter bottle, combine the vodka, vermouth, water and olive brine (if using). Cap the bottle securely, then shake to mix. Store in the freezer. To serve, pour into a cocktail glass and garnish with skewered olives for stirring.

Thirsty for more?
If you have some vodka to spare, try a:

Cancan REFRESHING | STRONG

MAKES 1 COCKTAIL

2 ounces (60 ml) vodka

¾ teaspoon (4 ml) agave or simple syrup

Dash Angostura bitters

Lemon zest strip

Ice cubes

2 ounces (60 ml) sparkling wine

In a rocks glass, combine the vodka, syrup, bitters and lemon zest. Stir gently with 1 large or 2 standard ice cubes. Top with sparkling wine.

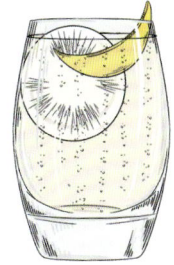

RUM

Apple Pie Cocktail   FRUITY | STRONG | SWEET

Back in my college days, the Holy Grail of drinking was crafting something that tasted as much as possible like apple pie. Sophisticated we were not. Even when we did get close to hitting the mark, we often drank too much and couldn't remember what we'd mixed. Which is why I was intrigued by Harry Craddock's 1930s take on the Apple Pie Cocktail. Interestingly, his version makes no pretense to mimic apple flavor. It uses apricot brandy and grenadine to build gentle sweetness on a base of white rum and sweet vermouth. I'm not sure how apple-like it is, but I still would have appreciated it back in the day.

 STARTING WITH A FULL BOTTLE?
Pour off 12 ounces (360 ml).

MAKES 5 TO 7 COCKTAILS

- 13 ounces (390 ml) white rum
- 3½ ounces (105 ml) sweet vermouth
- 3½ ounces (105 ml) apricot brandy
- 2 ounces (60 ml) water
- 1¾ ounces (53 ml) grenadine

In a 750-milliliter bottle, combine the rum, sweet vermouth, apricot brandy, water and grenadine. Cap the bottle securely, then shake well to mix. Store in the freezer. To serve, pour into a coupe.

Thirsty for more?
If you have some white rum to spare, try an:

Apple Cream Pie STRONG | CREAMY | SWEET | FRUITY

MAKES 1 COCKTAIL

- 2 ounces (60 ml) white rum
- 1½ ounces (45 ml) apple juice
- ½ ounce (15 ml) Licor 43
- ½ ounce (15 ml) egg white
- 6 to 10 granules sea salt
- Ice cubes

In a cocktail shaker, combine the rum, apple juice, Licor 43, egg white and salt. Shake with ice cubes. Strain into a coupe.

Buttered Rum CREAMY | SWEET | FRUITY

This recipe turns the Hot Buttered Rum on its head. Traditionally, it is a warm cocktail in which a pat of butter is melted into a steaming blend of rum, apple juice and spices. That certainly won't work for the freezer! Plus, it limits this cocktail to cool weather. To give this wonderful flavor combination year-round appeal, I fat-wash aged rum with melted butter. Once the rum is infused, the butter solids are discarded, leaving behind only a rich, sweetly flavored liquor. For the freezer version, instead of hot apple juice, I finish the cocktail in the glass with a splash of cider.

 STARTING WITH A FULL BOTTLE?
Pour off 7 ounces (210 ml).
MAKES 5 TO 7 COCKTAILS

- 8 tbsp (113 g) butter, melted
- 18 ounces (540 ml) aged rum
- 2¼ ounces (68 ml) orange liqueur
- 2¼ ounces (68 ml) agave or simple syrup
- 2 ounces (60 ml) water
- Generous pinch grated nutmeg
- Apple cider, to serve

In a heat-proof liquid measuring cup with at least a 4-cup (2-pint or 1-liter) capacity, microwave the butter until melted. Add the rum, then let sit at room temperature, stirring often, for 10 minutes. Place in the freezer for 1 hour; the butter will solidify on top of the rum. Strain through a muslin-lined mesh sieve into a 750-milliliter bottle; discard the solids. Add the orange liqueur, syrup, water and nutmeg. Cap the bottle securely, then shake well to mix. Store in the freezer. To serve, shake the bottle (some sediment on the bottom is normal), then fill a cocktail glass two-thirds full. Top with 1 to 2 ounces (30 to 60 ml) cider.

Thirsty for more?
If you have some aged rum to spare, try a:

Parisian Blonde CREAMY | SWEET

MAKES 1 COCKTAIL
- 1¼ (38 ml) ounces orange liqueur
- 1 ounce (30 ml) aged rum
- ½ ounce (15 ml) double cream
- Dash orange bitters
- 6 to 10 granules sea salt
- Ice cubes

In a cocktail shaker, combine the orange liqueur, rum, cream, bitters and salt. Shake with ice cubes, then strain into a cocktail glass.

Cinnamon Nut Bread CREAMY | STRONG | FRUITY

This is the dessert cocktail of your dreams! If you like cinnamon-spiked banana bread, and if you like booze... Well, this is going to do it for you. I use macadamia nuts because they add a creamy richness. But if you prefer, substitute cashews or even almonds. Avoid peanuts, which have a strong flavor that would overwhelm the other ingredients.

STARTING WITH A FULL BOTTLE?
Pour off 5 ounces (150 ml).

MAKES 5 TO 7 COCKTAILS

20 ounces (600 ml) white rum

¾ cup (4 oz, 115 g) macadamia nuts

Generous pinch ground cinnamon

2 ounces (60 ml) water

1½ ounces (45 ml) agave or simple syrup

¼ teaspoon (2 ml) Angostura bitters

Crushed ice, to serve

In a blender, combine the rum, nuts and cinnamon. Pulse until finely chopped but not pureed. Let sit for 3 minutes. Strain through a muslin-lined mesh sieve into a 750-milliliter bottle; discard the solids. Add the water, syrup and bitters. Cap the bottle securely, then shake well to mix. Store in the freezer. To serve, shake the bottle (some sediment on the bottom is normal), then pour into a coupe filled halfway with crushed ice.

Thirsty for more?
If you have some white rum to spare, try a:

Caribbean Christmas CREAMY | WARM | SPICY | SWEET

MAKES 1 COCKTAIL

3 ounces (90 ml) white rum

1 ounce (30 ml) coconut water

½ ounce (15 ml) orange liqueur

½ ounce (15 ml) egg white

¼ ounce (8 ml) agave or simple syrup

Pinch ground cinnamon

Ice cubes

In a cocktail shaker, combine the rum, coconut water, orange liqueur, egg white, syrup and cinnamon. Shake with ice cubes. Strain into a coupe.

Coconut-Lime Daiquiri Colada CREAMY | STRONG | SOUR | SWEET

This snappy little number straddles the line between a Lime Daiquiri and a Piña Colada. We start by speed infusing white rum with lime zest, producing a liquor that is bright and citrusy without being overwhelmingly acidic. Next, the infused rum is fat-washed with coconut oil, which adds a pronounced but not heavy richness that is the perfect complement to the sweet rum and tangy lime. You will need two squares of muslin.

 **STARTING WITH A FULL BOTTLE?**
Pour off 4 ounces (120 ml).
MAKES 5 TO 7 COCKTAILS

- 21 ounces (630 ml) white rum
- Zest strips from 2 limes
- 2 ounces (60 ml) coconut oil, melted
- 2 ounces (60 ml) water
- 2 ounces (60 ml) agave or simple syrup
- Crushed ice, to serve

In a blender, combine the rum and lime zest. Pulse until finely chopped but not pureed. Let sit for 3 minutes. Strain the rum through a muslin-lined mesh sieve into a liquid measuring cup with at least a 4-cup (2-pint or 1-liter) capacity. Discard the zest. Stir the melted coconut oil into the rum. Let sit at room temperature for 5 minutes, stirring often. Place in the freezer for 30 minutes. Strain again through a muslin-lined mesh sieve into a 750-milliliter bottle; discard the solids. Add the water and syrup. Cap the bottle securely, then shake well to mix. Store in the freezer. To serve, pour into a coupe filled halfway with crushed ice.

Thirsty for more?
If you have some white rum to spare, try a:

Frothed and Fruity FRUITY | REFRESHING | CREAMY

MAKES 1 COCKTAIL

- 3 ounces (90 ml) white rum
- 1 ounce (30 ml) mango juice
- 1 ounce (30 ml) coconut water
- ½ ounce (15 ml) egg white
- ¼ ounce (8 ml) lime juice
- Ice, cubes and crushed

In a cocktail shaker, combine the rum, mango juice, coconut water, egg white and lime juice. Shake with ice cubes. Strain into a rocks glass filled two-thirds with crushed ice.

Daiquiri SWEET | STRONG | SOUR

The simplicity of the Daiquiri—white rum, lime juice and sugar—makes it ideal for the freezer. Here I tinker with the typical proportions of almost equal parts lime and sugar. I find that a bit overwhelming whether a Daiquiri is destined for the freezer or not. I also like the balancing herbal notes of a dash of Peychaud's bitters, but feel free to leave that out. One note about the citrus: it tends to settle to the bottom of the bottle over time. So with the Daiquiri—or any citrusy freezer cocktail—give the bottle a good shake before serving.

 STARTING WITH A FULL BOTTLE?
Pour off 7 ounces (210 ml).
MAKES 5 TO 7 COCKTAILS

- 18 ounces (540 ml) white rum
- 2 ounces (60 ml) lime juice
- 2 ounces (60 ml) water
- 1¾ ounces (53 ml) agave or simple syrup
- ¼ teaspoon (2 ml) Peychaud's bitters (optional)
- Lime round, to serve

In a 750-milliliter bottle, combine the rum, lime juice, water, syrup and bitters, if using. Cap the bottle securely, then shake well to mix. Store in the freezer. To serve, shake again, then pour into a coupe and garnish with a lime round.

Thirsty for more?
If you have some white rum to spare, try a:

Navy Grog SWEET | SOUR | REFRESHING

MAKES 1 COCKTAIL

- 1½ ounces (45 ml) white rum
- 1½ ounces (45 ml) aged rum
- ½ ounce (15 ml) honey
- ½ ounce (15 ml) grapefruit juice
- ¼ ounce (8 ml) lime juice
- Ice cubes

In a cocktail shaker, combine the white rum, aged rum, honey, grapefruit juice and lime juice. Shake with ice cubes, then strain into a coupe.

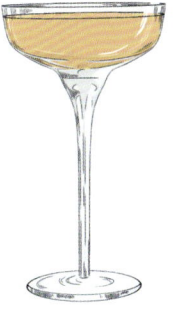

Mai Tai REFRESHING | SWEET | CREAMY

Fresh mint doesn't take kindly to the freezer, but it is a key component of a Mai Tai. So adapting this one to the freezer required some creativity. Purists will argue whether white or aged rum is best, but I prefer a blend. If you favor one over the other, then use your preferred rum; the recipe will work regardless. As for that mint, I settled on mint bitters. It's an easy way to add tons of flavor without worrying about freezing. And, of course, feel free to still garnish with a fresh mint sprig. Orgeat syrup is traditional, but you also can substitute agave or simple syrup.

 STARTING WITH A FULL BOTTLE?
Pour off 15 ounces (450 ml).
MAKES 5 TO 7 COCKTAILS

10 ounces (300 ml) white rum

7 ounces (210 ml) aged rum

4 ounces (120 ml) orange liqueur

1¾ ounces (53 ml) lime juice

1¾ ounces (53 ml) orgeat syrup

¼ teaspoon (2 ml) mint bitters

Crushed ice, to serve

Fresh mint sprigs, to serve

In a 750-milliliter bottle, combine the white rum, aged rum, orange liqueur, lime juice, syrup and bitters. Cap the bottle securely, then shake well to mix. Store in the freezer. To serve, pour into a highball or tiki glass filled halfway with crushed ice. Garnish with a mint sprig.

Thirsty for more?
If you have some white rum to spare, try a:

Rum Punch FRUITY | SOUR | SWEET | STRONG

MAKES 1 COCKTAIL

Lime slice, ¼ inch thick

½ ounce (15 ml) Campari

¼ ounce (8 ml) agave or simple syrup

3 ounces (90 ml) white rum

2 ounces (60 ml) pineapple juice

Ice cubes

Lime zest twist

In a cocktail shaker, muddle the lime slice, Campari and syrup. Add the rum and pineapple juice. Shake with ice cubes. Strain into a coupe. Garnish with the lime zest twist.

Mojito   REFRESHING | SWEET | HERBAL | SOUR

Cocktails that call for muddled fresh herbs present a problem for freezer adaptations. Luckily, for a mojito, mint bitters are an easy substitute that adds tons of flavor without risk of freezing. But don't skip the mint sprig to garnish, and be sure to give it a good smack between your hands before adding it to the glass. This enhances the drink with the minty aromatics that are so important to enjoying it.

 STARTING WITH A FULL BOTTLE?
Pour off 7 ounces (210 ml).

MAKES 5 TO 7 COCKTAILS

18 ounces (540 ml) white rum

3 ounces (90 ml) lime juice

2 ounces (60 ml) agave or simple syrup

¼ teaspoon (2 ml) mint bitters

Crushed ice, to serve

Mint sprigs, to garnish

In a 750-milliliter bottle, combine the rum, lime juice, syrup and bitters. Cap the bottle securely, then shake well to mix. Store in the freezer. To serve, pour into a highball glass filled halfway with crushed ice. Smack a mint sprig and add to the glass.

Thirsty for more?
If you have some white rum to spare, try a:

Zombie STRONG | HERBAL | SWEET

MAKES 1 COCKTAIL

1½ ounces (45 ml) white rum

1½ ounces (45 ml) aged rum

½ ounce (15 ml) pineapple juice

¼ ounce (8 ml) falernum syrup

¼ ounce (8 ml) grenadine

Scant pinch ground cinnamon

Dash Angostura bitters

Dash absinthe

6 to 10 granules sea salt

Ice, cubes and crushed

In a cocktail shaker, combine both rums, the pineapple juice, falernum syrup, grenadine, cinnamon, bitters, absinthe and salt. Shake with ice cubes, then strain into a highball glass filled two-thirds with crushed ice.

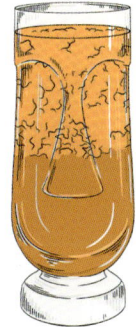

Poker Cocktail WARM | STRONG | SWEET

The Poker Cocktail is rum's answer to the Manhattan, combining sweet vermouth and bitters with white rum. Classic versions call for equal parts white rum and sweet vermouth, but my recipe favors the rum. This cocktail takes kindly to the freezer, so feel free to dial down the rum for more sweet vermouth. And while not conventional, if you want to push this cocktail even further along the Manhattan continuum, substitute aged rum for the white.

STARTING WITH A FULL BOTTLE?
Pour off 11 ounces (330 ml).

MAKES 5 TO 7 COCKTAILS

- 14 ounces (420 ml) white rum
- 7 ounces (210 ml) sweet vermouth
- 2 ounces (60 ml) water
- 1½ ounces (45 ml) agave or simple syrup
- ¼ teaspoon (2 ml) Angostura bitters
- Ice cubes, to serve

In a 750-milliliter bottle, combine the rum, vermouth, water, syrup and bitters. Cap the bottle securely, then shake well to mix. Store in the freezer. To serve, pour into a rocks glass with 1 large or 2 standard ice cubes.

Thirsty for more?
If you have some white rum to spare, try a:

Rumhattan STRONG | SWEET | BITTER | SPICY | SMOKY

MAKES 1 COCKTAIL

- 3 ounces (90 ml) white rum
- 1 ounce (30 ml) sweet vermouth
- 1 maraschino cherry
- Dash orange bitters
- Splash ginger beer
- Crushed ice

In a rocks glass, combine the rum, vermouth, cherry, bitters, ginger beer and crushed ice. Stir.

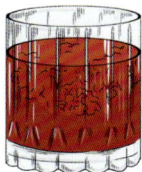

Rum Daisy   CREAMY | SOUR | HERBAL

We're going old-school Margarita! The basic Daisy is the precursor of the contemporary Margarita (which translates to "daisy"). Most recipes consist of some base liquor plus citrus juice and orange liqueur. Over the years, Daisies have been made with pretty much any bottle you care to imagine, but gin, whiskey and rum are most common. In this rum version, lemon juice is classically used. We skip that in favor of a lemon zest speed infusion for the rum. The flavor is cleaner, brighter and wonderfully floral.

 STARTING WITH A FULL BOTTLE?
Pour off 9 ounces (270 ml).
MAKES 5 TO 7 COCKTAILS

- 16 ounces (480 ml) white rum
- Zest strips from 1 lemon
- 4 ounces (120 ml) Yellow Chartreuse
- 3 ounces (90 ml) water
- 1½ ounces (45 ml) agave or simple syrup

In a blender, combine the rum and lemon zest. Pulse until the zest is finely chopped but not pureed. Let sit for 3 minutes. Strain through a muslin-lined mesh sieve into a 750-milliliter bottle. Add the Yellow Chartreuse, water and syrup. Cap the bottle securely, then shake well to mix. Store in the freezer. To serve, pour into a Nick and Nora glass.

Thirsty for more?
If you have some white rum to spare, try a:

Coconut-Lime Daiquiri CREAMY | STRONG | SOUR

MAKES 1 COCKTAIL

- 3 ounces (90 ml) white rum
- 1 ounce (30 ml) coconut milk
- ½ ounce (15 ml) lime juice
- ½ ounce (15 ml) agave or simple syrup
- 6 to 10 granules sea salt
- Ice cubes

In a cocktail shaker, combine the white rum, coconut milk, lime juice, syrup and salt. Shake with ice cubes, then strain into a rocks glass with 1 large or 2 standard ice cubes.

Tropical Coconut Pie CREAMY | SWEET | STRONG

This one is for summer. And any time you're in the mood for something a little trashy. Lean into it. You're going to take white rum and coconut rum and infuse them with lime zest. Then you're going to add coconut water. Are you feeling tropical yet? Throw in some orange bitters, because why not? Pop that sucker in the freezer, then grab a lounge chair by the pool. That is the vibe.

STARTING WITH A FULL BOTTLE?
Pour off 14½ ounces (435 ml).

MAKES 5 TO 7 COCKTAILS

- 10½ ounces (315 ml) white rum
- 10½ ounces (315 ml) coconut rum
- Zest strips from 1 lime
- Pinch sea salt
- 4 ounces (120 ml) coconut water
- Lime rounds, to serve

In a blender, combine the white rum, coconut rum, lime zest strips and salt. Pulse until the zest is finely chopped but not pureed. Let sit for 3 minutes. Strain through a muslin-lined mesh sieve into a 750-milliliter bottle. Add the coconut water. Cap the bottle securely, then shake well to mix. Store in the freezer. To serve, pour into a cocktail glass and garnish with a lime round.

Thirsty for more?
If you have some white rum to spare, try a:

Lime Cream Pie CREAMY | SOUR | SWEET

MAKES 1 COCKTAIL

- 3 ounces (90 ml) white rum
- 1½ ounces (45 ml) coconut water
- 1 tablespoon (15 ml) plain fat-free Greek yogurt
- ¼ ounce (8 ml) lime juice
- ¼ ounce (8 ml) agave or simple syrup
- Ice cubes

In a cocktail shaker, combine the rum, coconut water, yogurt, lime juice and syrup. Shake with ice cubes. Strain into a coupe.

GIN

Alaska Cocktail STRONG | HERBAL | SWEET

This bracing botanical cocktail will bring a touch of sophistication to your freezer. Ha! Who am I kidding? You're going to line up shot glasses of this pretty little number—a relative of the Gin Martini that gets complicated thanks to Yellow Chartreuse and orange bitters—and do them before your book club. Or pool party. Or Netflix and chill. Whatever.

STARTING WITH A FULL BOTTLE?
Pour off 10 ounces (300 ml).

MAKES 5 TO 7 COCKTAILS

- 15 ounces (450 ml) gin
- 4 ounces (120 ml) Yellow Chartreuse
- 3 ounces (90 ml) water
- ¼ teaspoon (2 ml) orange bitters
- Crushed ice, to serve
- Lemon zest strips, to serve

In a 750-milliliter bottle, combine the gin, Yellow Chartreuse, water and bitters. Cap the bottle securely, then shake well to mix. Store in the freezer. To serve, pour into a Nick and Nora glass filled halfway with crushed ice. Rub a lemon zest strip around the rim of the glass, then add it to the drink.

Thirsty for more?
If you have some gin to spare, try a:

Gin Daisy SOUR | SWEET | HERBAL

MAKES 1 COCKTAIL

- 2 ounces (60 ml) gin
- ½ ounce (15 ml) Yellow Chartreuse
- ¼ ounce (8 ml) grenadine
- ¾ teaspoon (4 ml) lemon juice
- ¾ teaspoon (4 ml) lime juice
- Ice cubes

In a stirring glass, combine the gin, Chartreuse, grenadine and both juices. Stir with ice cubes, then strain into a cocktail glass.

Aviation   CREAMY | SPICY | SWEET

The classic Aviation is a floral mix of gin, maraschino liqueur, crème de violette and a whole lot of lemon juice. I've never been a fan of the original because the lemon and crème de violette overwhelm the other ingredients. My version tames the unruly elements by using lemon zest instead of juice—you keep the bright citrus notes without adding all that acid, and you put it directly in the glass, so there's no worry about the juice freezing—and ditches the perfume-like crème de violette for a lightly sweet, gently spicy blend of Lillet Blanc and Bénédictine. A far more sophisticated way to fly.

 STARTING WITH A FULL BOTTLE?
Pour off 11 ounces (330 ml).
MAKES 5 TO 7 COCKTAILS

- 14 ounces (420 ml) gin
- 3½ ounces (105 ml) Bénédictine
- 2 ounces (60 ml) water
- 1¾ ounces (53 ml) maraschino liqueur
- 1¾ ounces (53 ml) Lillet Blanc
- ¼ teaspoon (2 ml) Angostura bitters
- Ice cubes, to serve
- Lemon zest strips, to serve

In a 750-milliliter bottle, combine the gin, Bénédictine, water, maraschino liqueur, Lillet Blanc and bitters. Cap the bottle securely, then shake well to mix. Store in the freezer. To serve, pour into a rocks glass with 1 large or 2 standard ice cubes. Rub a lemon zest strip around the rim of the glass, then add to the drink.

Thirsty for more?
If you have some gin to spare, try a:

Pegu Club Cocktail CREAMY | STRONG

MAKES 1 COCKTAIL

- 1 lime zest strip
- 2 ounces (60 ml) gin
- ½ ounce (15 ml) orange liqueur
- ½ ounce (15 ml) dry vermouth
- ¾ teaspoon (4 ml) agave or simple syrup
- Dash Angostura bitters
- Dash orange bitters
- 6 to 10 granules sea salt
- Ice cubes

Rub the lime zest strip around the rim of a coupe, then add it to the glass. In a cocktail shaker, combine the gin, orange liqueur, dry vermouth, syrup, both bitters and salt. Shake with ice cubes, then strain into the coupe.

Bijou HERBAL | WARM | CREAMY

The Bijou is gin's answer to a Manhattan or Old Fashioned, and it's an easy adaptation for the freezer. The botanicals of the gin are lightly sweetened by the vermouth, with an herbal boost from the Green Chartreuse. Bitters, particularly the orange, give the cocktail balance with some gentle fruity notes.

STARTING WITH A FULL BOTTLE?
Pour off 13 ounces (390 ml).

MAKES 5 TO 7 COCKTAILS

- 12 ounces (360 ml) gin
- 6 ounces (180 ml) sweet vermouth
- 3 ounces (90 ml) Green Chartreuse
- 2 ounces (60 ml) water
- ¼ teaspoon (2 ml) Angostura bitters
- ¼ teaspoon (2 ml) orange bitters
- Ice cubes, to serve

In a 750-milliliter bottle, combine the gin, vermouth, Green Chartreuse, water and both bitters. Cap the bottle securely, then shake well to mix. Store in the freezer. To serve, pour into a rocks glass with 1 large or 2 standard ice cubes.

Thirsty for more?
If you have some gin to spare, try a:

Lychee-Mint Martini
CREAMY | STRONG | SWEET | HERBAL

MAKES 1 COCKTAIL

- 3 lychee fruit (canned in juice)
- 2 sprigs fresh mint
- 3 ounces (90 ml) gin
- ¼ ounce (8 ml) agave or simple syrup
- Dash orange bitters
- Ice, cubes and crushed

In a cocktail shaker, muddle the lychees and 1 mint sprig. Add the gin, syrup and bitters. Shake with ice cubes. Double strain into a coupe filled halfway with crushed ice. Smack the remaining mint sprig and garnish the cocktail with it.

Blue Moon Cocktail FRUITY | HERBAL | SWEET

This is the bottled cocktail you haul to the beach or pool. Blue like the azure ripples of the water, this fruity and sweet mix goes down smoothly. If you don't have both crème de violette and Blue Curaçao, use a double dose of one or the other. Many traditional recipes actually call for that, but I favor the fruity blend of both. I suggest sipping it from a cocktail glass with a generous dose of crushed ice, though if you're feeling the party vibe, doing shots off a fellow partygoer's taut abs works, too.

 STARTING WITH A FULL BOTTLE?
Pour off 9 ounces (270 ml).

MAKES 5 TO 7 COCKTAILS

- 16 ounces (480 ml) gin
- Zest strips from 1 lemon, plus strips to serve
- 3½ ounces (105 ml) crème de violette
- 3 ounces (90 ml) water
- 1¾ ounces (53 ml) Blue Curaçao
- Crushed ice, to serve

In a blender, combine the gin and zest strips from 1 lemon. Pulse until the zest is finely chopped but not pureed. Let sit for 3 minutes. Strain the gin through a muslin-lined mesh sieve into a 750-milliliter bottle. Add the crème de violette, water and Blue Curaçao. Cap the bottle securely, then shake well to mix. Store in the freezer. To serve, pour into a cocktail glass filled halfway with crushed ice. Rub a lemon zest strip around the rim of the glass, then discard the zest.

Thirsty for more?
If you have some gin to spare, try an:

Inca   SWEET | STRONG | FRUITY

MAKES 1 COCKTAIL

- 1 ounce (30 ml) gin
- 1 ounce (30 ml) dry sherry
- 1 ounce (30 ml) dry vermouth
- ¾ teaspoon (4 ml) orgeat syrup
- Dash orange bitters
- Ice cubes
- 1 chunk fresh pineapple

In a cocktail shaker, combine the gin, sherry, vermouth, orgeat and bitters. Shake with ice cubes, then strain into a coupe and add the pineapple on a cocktail skewer.

Chocolate Negroni BITTER | CREAMY | HERBAL

Bittersweet cocoa goodness with freezer ease. You are welcome. This rich and creamy take on the classically bitter Italian Negroni originated with New York City mixologist Naren Young. The addition of crème de cacao and Punt e Mes, an Italian vermouth that is a bit like sweet vermouth crossed with an amaro, creates a cocktail reminiscent of the original, but with a whole new depth.

 STARTING WITH A FULL BOTTLE?
Pour off 17 ounces (510 ml).
MAKES 5 TO 7 COCKTAILS

8 ounces (240 ml) gin

6 ounces (180 ml) Punt e Mes

6 ounces (180 ml) Campari

2 ounces (60 ml) water

1½ ounces (45 ml) crème de cacao

¼ teaspoon (2 ml) chocolate bitters

Ice cubes, to serve

In a 750-milliliter bottle, combine the gin, Punt e Mes, Campari, water, crème de cacao and bitters. Cap the bottle securely, then shake well to mix. Store in the freezer. To serve, pour into a rocks glass with 1 large or 2 standard ice cubes.

Thirsty for more?
If you have some gin to spare, try an:

Up and at 'Em   CREAMY | FRUITY | SWEET

MAKES 1 COCKTAIL

2 ounces (60 ml) gin

½ ounce (15 ml) orange liqueur

½ ounce (15 ml) white rum

¼ ounce (8 ml) agave or simple syrup

Dash orange bitters

Dash Angostura bitters

6 to 10 granules sea salt

Ice cubes

Orange zest twist

In a cocktail shaker, combine the gin, orange liqueur, rum, syrup, both bitters and salt. Shake with ice cubes. Strain into a rocks glass and garnish with the orange zest twist.

Cinnamon Toast Martini WARM | SWEET | REFRESHING | CREAMY

This cocktail tastes just like its name suggests—warm, spicy and a little sweet. Go ahead and pour one for breakfast. I won't tell. Though my recipe calls for gin, this cocktail is also delicious—if a little less complex—made with vodka. Whatever gets your morning going.

STARTING WITH A FULL BOTTLE?
Pour off 7 ounces (210 ml).

MAKES 5 TO 7 COCKTAILS

- 18 ounces (540 ml) gin
- 3 ounces (90 ml) water
- 1½ ounces (45 ml) agave or simple syrup
- ¼ teaspoon (2 ml) orange bitters
- Pinch ground cinnamon
- Crushed ice, to serve

In a 750-milliliter bottle, combine the gin, water, syrup, bitters and cinnamon. Cap the bottle securely, then shake well to mix. Store in the freezer. To serve, shake well, then pour into a cocktail glass filled halfway with crushed ice.

Thirsty for more?
If you have some gin to spare, try a:

Gin Fizz CREAMY | REFRESHING | SOUR | SWEET

MAKES 1 COCKTAIL

- 3 ounces (90 ml) gin
- ½ ounce (15 ml) egg white
- ¼ ounce (8 ml) orange liqueur
- ¼ ounce (8 ml) lemon juice
- ¼ ounce (8 ml) lime juice
- ¼ ounce (8 ml) agave or simple syrup
- 6 to 10 granules sea salt
- Ice cubes
- Splash carbonated water

In a cocktail shaker, combine the gin, egg white, orange liqueur, lemon juice, lime juice, syrup and salt. Dry shake without ice for 20 seconds. Add ice cubes, then shake for 10 seconds. Strain into a coupe, then add a splash of carbonated water.

Damn-the-Weather Cocktail HERBAL | FRUITY | SWEET

This citrusy and botanical Prohibition-era cocktail traditionally calls for fresh orange juice combined with gin, sweet vermouth and orange liqueur. But I've never been much of a fan of orange juice in cocktails. The pulp tends to leave everything a little gunky. So for this update, I use orange zest to infuse the gin. The result is bright, clean orange flavor without the messy bits.

STARTING WITH A FULL BOTTLE?
Pour off 11 ounces (330 ml).

MAKES 5 TO 7 COCKTAILS

14 ounces (420 ml) gin

Zest strips from 1 orange

½ ounce (15 ml) agave or simple syrup

Pinch sea salt

6¾ ounces (203 ml) sweet vermouth

2¼ ounces (68 ml) orange liqueur

1 ounce (30 ml) water

In a blender, combine the gin, orange zest, syrup and salt. Pulse until the zest is finely chopped but not pureed. Let sit for 3 minutes. Strain through a muslin-lined mesh sieve into a 750-milliliter bottle. Add the sweet vermouth, orange liqueur and water. Cap the bottle securely, then shake well to mix. Store in the freezer. To serve, pour into a coupe.

Thirsty for more?
If you have some gin to spare, try:

The Poet's Dream

CREAMY | FRUITY | REFRESHING | STRONG

MAKES 1 COCKTAIL

1 orange zest strip

2 ounces (60 ml) gin

¾ ounce (23 ml) dry vermouth

½ ounce (15 ml) Bénédictine

¾ teaspoon (4 ml) orgeat syrup

Dash orange bitters

Ice cubes

Rub the zest around the rim of a coupe, then add it to the glass. In a cocktail shaker, combine the gin, vermouth, Bénédictine, orgeat syrup and bitters. Shake with ice cubes. Strain into the coupe.

Gin Martini STRONG | HERBAL

Though many people consider the Gin Martini the platonic form of Martinis, it has gone through many changes over the years. Born sometime during the late 1800s, it has been shaken and stirred. It has been dry (dry vermouth and gin, nothing more), medium (a blend of sweet and dry vermouths) and sweet (sweet vermouth only). Green olives were a common garnish. Orange bitters also were (and remain) a frequent flyer. After sifting and tasting my way through the history, I've gone back to basics. A simple stir of gin, dry vermouth and orange bitters. If you like it a little dirty, add the optional olive brine (or just add that to your serving glass along with the olives).

 STARTING WITH A FULL BOTTLE?
Pour off 7½ ounces (225 ml).
MAKES 5 TO 7 COCKTAILS

- 17½ ounces (525 ml) gin
- 3½ ounces (105 ml) dry vermouth
- 3 ounces (90 ml) water
- ½ to 1 ounce (15 to 30 ml) green olive brine (optional)
- ¼ teaspoon (2 ml) orange bitters
- Green olives, to serve

In a 750-milliliter bottle, combine the gin, vermouth, water, brine (if using) and bitters. Cap the bottle securely, then shake well to mix. Store in the freezer. To serve, pour into a cocktail glass and garnish with green olives on a cocktail skewer.

Thirsty for more?
If you have some gin to spare, try a:

1920 Pick-Me-Up STRONG | HERBAL | FRUITY | SWEET

MAKES 1 COCKTAIL

- 3 ounces (90 ml) gin
- ¾ teaspoon (4 ml) absinthe
- ¾ teaspoon (4 ml) gum syrup or simple syrup
- Dash Angostura bitters
- Dash orange bitters
- Ice cubes

In a cocktail shaker, combine the gin, absinthe, syrup and both bitters. Shake with ice cubes, then strain into a Nick and Nora glass.

Hanky-Panky HERBAL | STRONG | SWEET

This is the bottle for a night of brooding with a book by the fire. A sweet and strong little number, it's a relative of the Horse Thief, with bitter Fernet-Branca amaro replacing the absinthe. Credit for its creation in the early 1900s goes to Ada Coleman of the American Bar at the Savoy Hotel in London. She made it for a frequent customer fond of asking for a drink with "a bit of punch in it." Apparently, when the customer first tasted this cocktail, he responded with "By Jove! That is the real hanky-panky!"

 STARTING WITH A FULL BOTTLE?
Pour off 9 ounces (270 ml).
MAKES 5 TO 7 COCKTAILS

16 ounces (480 ml) gin

4 ounces (120 ml) sweet vermouth

2 ounces (60 ml) water

1 ounce (30 ml) Fernet-Branca amaro

Orange zest strip, to serve

In a 750-milliliter bottle, combine the gin, sweet vermouth, water and Fernet-Branca. Cap the bottle securely, then shake well to mix. Store in the freezer. To serve, pour into a coupe. Rub an orange zest strip around the rim of the glass, then add to the glass.

Thirsty for more?
If you have some gin to spare, try a:

Gin and It SPICY | SWEET | CREAMY | STRONG

MAKES 1 COCKTAIL

1 orange zest strip

2 ounces (60 ml) gin

1 ounce (30 ml) sweet vermouth

Dash Angostura bitters

Ice cubes

1 maraschino cherry

Rub the zest strip around the rim of a rocks glass, then add it to the glass. In a stirring glass, combine the gin, sweet vermouth and bitters. Stir with ice cubes, then strain into the rocks glass and add the cherry.

The Horse Thief HERBAL | STRONG | SWEET

This smooth yet complex cocktail was created by Tom Bullock, the first Black bartender to publish a cocktail book. *The Ideal Bartender* was released in 1917, and its 173 recipes set the standard for decades to come. His Horse Thief was a stirred blend of absinthe, sweet vermouth and gin, a combination with depth and gentle sweetness. With the addition of just a splash of water, it becomes the perfect sophisticated sipper to keep in the freezer.

STARTING WITH A FULL BOTTLE?
Pour off 12 ounces (360 ml).
MAKES 5 TO 7 COCKTAILS

- 13 ounces (390 ml) gin
- 7 ounces (210 ml) sweet vermouth
- 2 ounces (60 ml) water
- 1¾ ounces (53 ml) absinthe

In a 750-milliliter bottle, combine the gin, sweet vermouth, water and absinthe. Cap the bottle securely, then shake well to mix. Store in the freezer. To serve, pour into a cocktail glass.

Thirsty for more?
If you have some gin to spare, try:

The Sidearm

SWEET | REFRESHING | SOUR | HERBAL | STRONG

MAKES 1 COCKTAIL

- 2 ounces (60 ml) gin
- 1½ ounces (45 ml) brandy
- ¼ ounce (8 ml) lemon juice
- ¼ ounce (8 ml) agave or simple syrup
- Dash orange bitters
- 1 sprig fresh rosemary, smacked
- Ice cubes

In a cocktail shaker, combine the gin, brandy, lemon juice, syrup, bitters and rosemary. Shake with ice cubes. Strain into a coupe. Fish the rosemary out of the shaker and toss it into the glass.

Kiss in the Dark   SWEET | FRUITY | HERBAL

Time to trot out the flirty-fruity side of your freezer! This pink lady traditionally is made from equal parts gin, dry vermouth and cherry brandy. But the cherry can overwhelm, so I tamp it down and lean in with the gin and dry vermouth. If you prefer particularly sweet kisses, go ahead and make this with equal parts. Since this recipe calls for equal parts of two liquors, consider building it in an empty bottle.

 STARTING WITH A FULL BOTTLE?
Pour off 17 ounces (510 ml).

MAKES 5 TO 7 COCKTAILS

- 8 ounces (240 ml) gin
- 8 ounces (240 ml) dry vermouth
- 4 ounces (120 ml) cherry brandy
- 3 ounces (90 ml) water
- 1 ounce (30 ml) agave or simple syrup
- ¼ teaspoon (2 ml) Peychaud's bitters

In a 750-milliliter bottle, combine the gin, dry vermouth, cherry brandy, water, syrup and bitters. Cap the bottle securely, then shake well to mix. Store in the freezer. To serve, pour into a Nick and Nora glass.

Thirsty for more?
If you have some gin to spare, try:

The Monkey Gland SWEET | FRUITY | SOUR | HERBAL

MAKES 1 COCKTAIL

- ¼ teaspoon (½ gram) fennel seeds
- ¼ ounce (8 ml) grenadine
- 3 ounces (90 ml) gin
- ½ ounce (15 ml) pulp-free orange juice
- ¼ ounce (8 ml) Licor 43
- Dash Angostura bitters
- 6 to 10 granules sea salt
- Ice cubes

In a cocktail shaker, muddle the fennel seeds with the grenadine. Leave the muddler in the shaker. Add the gin, orange juice, Licor 43, bitters and salt. Swish the muddler to rinse it, then remove. Shake with ice cubes, then double strain into a coupe.

The Last Word STRONG | HERBAL | FRUITY | SWEET

Just shut up and drink! That's the vibe I've always associated with the Last Word. One part strong and herbal gin cocktail, one part laid-back attitude. The original dates to around Prohibition at the Detroit Athletic Club and was made with equal parts gin, Green Chartreuse, maraschino liqueur and lime juice. I ditch the lime because it turns the drink into a sweet-and-sour bomb. My version keeps the chill vibe going with the addition of Licor 43, which brings spicy vanilla notes to the game. It's usually served without ice, but I found it benefits from a little crushed ice.

STARTING WITH A FULL BOTTLE?
Pour off 10 ounces (300 ml).
MAKES 5 TO 7 COCKTAILS

- 15 ounces (450 ml) gin
- 3 ounces (90 ml) Green Chartreuse
- 3 ounces (90 ml) maraschino liqueur
- 2 ounces (60 ml) water
- 1¾ ounces (53 ml) Licor 43
- ¼ teaspoon (2 ml) Angostura bitters
- Crushed ice, to serve

In a 750-milliliter bottle, combine the gin, Green Chartreuse, maraschino liqueur, water, Licor 43 and bitters. Cap the bottle securely, then shake well to mix. Store in the freezer. To serve, pour into a coupe filled halfway with crushed ice.

Thirsty for more?
If you have some gin to spare, try a:

Golden Vesper STRONG | FRUITY

MAKES 1 COCKTAIL

- 2¼ ounces (68 ml) gin
- ¾ ounce (23 ml) vodka
- ½ ounce (15 ml) Licor 43
- Dash orange bitters
- Ice cubes
- Orange zest twist

In a stirring glass, stir the gin, vodka, Licor 43 and bitters with ice cubes. Strain into a coupe. Garnish with the orange zest twist.

Maiden's Blush   HERBAL | FRUITY | SOUR | SWEET

Not sure what she is blushing about, but if you drink enough of this bottle, I suspect you will be, too. Maybe right away. Maybe the next morning. As for the cocktail, it's the grenadine that gets you the requisite pink hue. Try to find real grenadine, which is made from pomegranate juice. Most of the cheaper stuff is just colored sugar water and adds no real flavor.

STARTING WITH A FULL BOTTLE?
Pour off 7 ounces (210 ml).

MAKES 5 TO 7 COCKTAILS

- 18 ounces (540 ml) gin
- Zest strips from 1 lemon
- Pinch sea salt
- 2½ ounces (75 ml) orange liqueur
- 2½ ounces (75 ml) grenadine
- 2 ounces (60 ml) water
- Crushed ice, to serve

In a blender, combine the gin, lemon zest and salt. Pulse until the zest is finely chopped but not pureed. Let sit for 3 minutes. Strain through a muslin-lined mesh sieve into a 750-milliliter bottle. Add the orange liqueur, grenadine and water. Cap the bottle securely, then shake well to mix. Store in the freezer. To serve, pour into a coupe filled halfway with crushed ice.

Thirsty for more?
If you have some gin to spare, try a:

Bee's Knees SWEET | SOUR | REFRESHING

MAKES 1 COCKTAIL

- ¼ ounce (8 ml) honey
- 2½ ounces (75 ml) gin
- ¼ ounce (8 ml) lemon juice
- ¼ ounce (8 ml) ginger liqueur
- Dash orange bitters
- 6 to 10 granules sea salt
- Ice, cubes and crushed

In a cocktail shaker, combine the honey, gin, lemon juice, ginger liqueur, bitters and salt. Shake with ice cubes. Strain into a rocks glass filled halfway with crushed ice.

Martinez STRONG | HERBAL | SWEET

This classic, which dates back to at least the mid-1800s, is a bit like a Manhattan in which gin stands in for rye. The resulting strong and sweet cocktail makes a lovely sipper. Many recipes also toss in some maraschino liqueur, but I prefer the brighter flavor of orange liqueur, a common substitute. I keep the cherry flavor by adding a maraschino cherry to the finished cocktail. Since this recipe calls for equal parts of two liquors, consider building it in an empty bottle.

 STARTING WITH A FULL BOTTLE?
Pour off 15 ounces (450 ml).
MAKES 5 TO 7 COCKTAILS

10 ounces (300 ml) gin

10 ounces (300 ml) sweet vermouth

2½ ounces (75 ml) water

1¾ ounces (53 ml) orange liqueur

¼ teaspoon (2 ml) Angostura bitters

Maraschino cherries, to serve

In a 750-milliliter bottle, combine the gin, sweet vermouth, water, orange liqueur and bitters. Cap the bottle securely, then shake well to mix. Store in the freezer. To serve, pour into a coupe and add a maraschino cherry.

Thirsty for more?
If you have some gin or sweet vermouth to spare, try a:

Make Your Mark   STRONG | HERBAL | BITTER | SWEET

MAKES 1 COCKTAIL

Orange zest strip

1½ ounces (45 ml) gin

1 ounce (30 ml) bourbon

½ ounce (15 ml) sweet vermouth

¼ ounce (8 ml) agave or simple syrup

Dash Angostura bitters

Ice cubes

Rub the orange zest strip around the rim of a coupe, then add it to the glass. In a stirring glass, combine the gin, bourbon, sweet vermouth, syrup and bitters. Stir with ice cubes. Strain into the coupe.

Negroni   BITTER | CREAMY | REFRESHING | FRUITY

The delightfully bittersweet Negroni is made from equal parts gin, Campari (an Italian liqueur similar to Aperol, but slightly more bitter) and sweet vermouth. With all that liquor, it's the perfect recipe for the freezer. I sometimes use a mix of ginger liqueur and orange liqueur in place of the sweet vermouth, but it's hard to beat the classic. The Negroni usually is served with an orange zest strip, a flavor I like to double down on with a bit of orange bitters, but that's optional. Since this recipe calls for equal parts of three liquors, consider building it in an empty bottle.

 STARTING WITH A FULL BOTTLE?
Pour off 17 ounces (510 ml).
MAKES 5 TO 7 COCKTAILS

- 8 ounces (240 ml) gin
- 8 ounces (240 ml) sweet vermouth
- 8 ounces (240 ml) Campari
- ¼ teaspoon (2 ml) orange bitters (optional)
- Ice cubes, to serve
- Orange zest strips, to serve

In a 750-milliliter bottle, combine the gin, sweet vermouth, Campari and bitters (if using). Cap the bottle securely, then shake well to mix. Store in the freezer. To serve, pour into a rocks glass with 1 large ice cube and an orange zest strip.

Thirsty for more?
If you have some gin to spare, try an:

Old Pal BITTER | SWEET | FRUITY | SOUR

MAKES 1 COCKTAIL
- 2 ounces (60 ml) gin
- ½ ounce (15 ml) Aperol
- ½ ounce (15 ml) grapefruit juice
- ¼ ounce (8 ml) elderflower liqueur
- 6 to 10 granules sea salt
- Ice cubes
- Lemon zest twist

In a cocktail shaker, combine the gin, Aperol, grapefruit juice, elderflower liqueur and salt. Shake with ice cubes, then strain into a coupe and garnish with the lemon zest twist.

Orange Martini STRONG | FRUITY

Orange Martini recipes are generally a sugary blend of flavored vodkas and coconut rum. At least today they are. But 100 years ago, it was a more sophisticated affair. And satisfying. Harry Craddock called for a simple Martini that blends gin, dry vermouth and sweet vermouth infused for two hours with orange zest. The mixture is strained and added to a glass rinsed with orange bitters. I speed up this equation for our deep-chill version. The blender makes quick work of the infusion and the zest is easily strained out before we bottle and freeze the cocktail. The result is a martini that is pleasantly dry, yet brightly fruity.

STARTING WITH A FULL BOTTLE?
Pour off 11 ounces (330 ml).
MAKES 5 TO 7 COCKTAILS

14 ounces (420 ml) gin

Zest strips from 1 orange, plus more to serve

1 ounce (30 ml) agave or simple syrup

Pinch sea salt

3½ ounces (105 ml) dry vermouth

3½ ounces (105 ml) sweet vermouth

3 ounces (90 ml) water

¼ teaspoon (2 ml) orange bitters

Crushed ice, to serve

In a blender, combine the gin, zest strips from 1 orange, syrup and salt. Pulse until the zest is finely chopped but not pureed. Let sit for 3 minutes. Strain through a muslin-lined mesh sieve into a 750-milliliter bottle; discard the zest. Add the dry vermouth, sweet vermouth, water and bitters. Cap the bottle securely, then shake well to mix. Store in the freezer. To serve, pour into a coupe filled halfway with crushed ice. Garnish with an orange zest strip on a cocktail skewer.

Thirsty for more?
If you have some gin to spare, try a:

Pendennis Club STRONG | FRUITY

MAKES 1 COCKTAIL

Lime zest strip

1½ ounces (45 ml) gin

¾ ounce (23 ml) apricot brandy

¾ ounce (23 ml) dry vermouth

Ice cubes

Rub the zest strip around the rim of a coupe, then discard the zest. In a cocktail shaker, combine the gin, brandy and vermouth. Shake with ice cubes, then strain into the glass.

Satan's Whiskers FRUITY | SWEET | STRONG

Bright, citrusy and sweet, Satan's Whiskers is a sassy blend of gin, orange liqueur and dry vermouth. Traditional recipes also toss in some sweet vermouth, which I find unnecessary, and sometimes orange juice and bitters. For the sake of the freezer—and a cleaner flavor—this recipe skips the juice, but keeps the bitters.

STARTING WITH A FULL BOTTLE?
Pour off 11 ounces (330 ml).

MAKES 5 TO 7 COCKTAILS

- 14 ounces (420 ml) gin
- 3½ ounces (105 ml) dry vermouth
- 3½ ounces (105 ml) orange liqueur
- 1 ounce (30 ml) agave or simple syrup
- ¼ teaspoon (2 ml) orange bitters
- Orange zest strips, to serve
- Crushed ice, to serve

In a 750-milliliter bottle, combine the gin, dry vermouth, orange liqueur, syrup and bitters. Cap the bottle securely, then shake well to mix. Store in the freezer. To serve, rub an orange zest strip around the rim of a coupe filled halfway with crushed ice. Add the zest to the glass, then pour in the cocktail.

Thirsty for more?
If you have some gin to spare, try a:

Drain the Swamp

REFRESHING | FRUITY | SWEET | SOUR | STRONG

MAKES 1 COCKTAIL

- 2 ounces (60 ml) gin
- 1 ounce (30 ml) sweet vermouth
- 1 ounce (30 ml) grapefruit juice
- ¼ ounce (8 ml) agave or simple syrup
- Dash Angostura bitters
- Ice cubes

In a cocktail shaker, combine the gin, vermouth, grapefruit juice, syrup and bitters. Shake with ice cubes. Strain into a coupe.

Vesper STRONG | SWEET

Even James Bond has a gentle side. Welcome to the Vesper, a softer, lightly refreshing take on the classic Gin Martini. And yes, you can thank Bond for it. The Vesper first appeared in Ian Fleming's 1953 James Bond novel *Casino Royale*. The dashing spy initially orders a dry Martini, then changes his mind and asks the bartender to make an unnamed cocktail that eventually came to be known as the Vesper. In addition to gin, it gets a hint of vodka and a generous dose of either Lillet Blanc or Cocchi Americano. Both are fruity fortified wines that complement the botanical notes of the gin.

 STARTING WITH A FULL BOTTLE?
Pour off 10 ounces (300 ml).
MAKES 5 TO 7 COCKTAILS

15 ounces (450 ml) gin

5 ounces (150 ml) Cocchi Americano or Lillet Blanc

2½ ounces (75 ml) vodka

2½ ounces (75 ml) water

In a 750-milliliter bottle, combine the gin, Cocchi Americano or Lillet Blanc, vodka and water. Cap the bottle securely, then shake well to mix. Store in the freezer. To serve, pour into a cocktail glass.

Thirsty for more?
If you have some gin to spare, try an:

Exposition Cocktail

STRONG | SWEET | FRUITY

MAKES 1 COCKTAIL

1 ounce (30 ml) gin

1 ounce (30 ml) dry vermouth

½ ounce (15 ml) cherry brandy

6 to 10 granules sea salt

Ice cubes

In a cocktail shaker, combine the gin, vermouth, brandy and salt. Shake with ice cubes, then strain into a cocktail glass.

AGAVE
(TEQUILA AND MEZCAL)

Amalfi Lemon Margarita STRONG | SWEET | CREAMY | SOUR

The classic Margarita calls for four things—tequila, orange liqueur, sugar and lime. This variation, inspired by a cocktail at Bitter & Twisted in Phoenix, keeps the key flavors, but gets to the finish line a little differently. Italian limoncello—a sweet, boldly lemony Italian liqueur—provides most of the sugar and all of the citrus. To give the cocktail creamy tropical notes that play perfectly with the limoncello, we use coconut oil to fat-wash the tequila. The result is wildly refreshing and tropical.

STARTING WITH A FULL BOTTLE?
Pour off 7½ ounces (225 ml).

MAKES 5 TO 7 COCKTAILS

- 17½ ounces (525 ml) blanco tequila
- 2 ounces (60 ml) coconut oil, melted
- 5¼ ounces (158 ml) limoncello
- 1 ounce (30 ml) agave or simple syrup
- Crushed ice, to serve

In a liquid measuring cup with at least a 4-cup (2-pint or 1-liter) capacity, stir together the tequila and coconut oil. Let sit at room temperature for 5 minutes, stirring often. Place in the freezer for 30 minutes. Strain through a muslin-lined mesh sieve into a 750-milliliter bottle; discard the solids. Add the limoncello and syrup. Cap the bottle securely, then shake well to mix. Store in the freezer. To serve, pour into a coupe filled halfway with crushed ice.

Thirsty for more?
If you have some blanco tequila to spare, try an:

Italian Margarita CREAMY | SWEET

MAKES 1 COCKTAIL

- 2½ ounces (75 ml) blanco tequila
- ¾ ounce (23 ml) limoncello
- ¾ ounce (23 ml) coconut water
- ¼ ounce (8 ml) agave syrup
- 6 to 10 granules sea salt
- Ice, cubes and crushed

In a cocktail shaker, combine the tequila, limoncello, coconut water, syrup and salt. Shake with ice cubes, then strain into a coupe filled halfway with crushed ice.

El Diablo FRUITY | REFRESHING

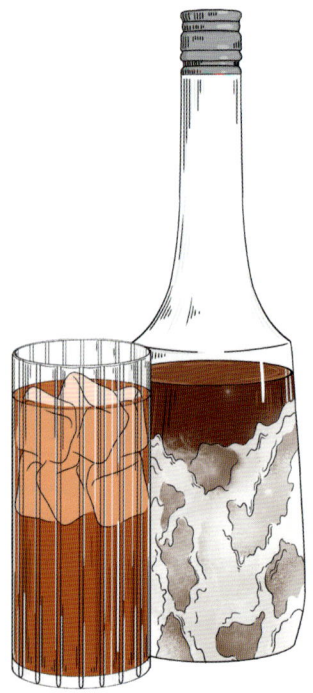

This nearly 100-year-old classic gets its spicy side from the ginger beer used to top it in the glass. But I also like to build some of that flavor right into the drink with a bit of ginger liqueur. Blackcurrant-flavored crème de cassis balances things with fruity sweetness.

 STARTING WITH A FULL BOTTLE?
Pour off 7 ounces (210 ml).

MAKES 8 COCKTAILS

- 18 ounces (540 ml) blanco tequila
- Zest strips from 1 lime
- 5 ounces (150 ml) crème de cassis
- 2 ounces (60 ml) ginger liqueur
- Ice cubes, to serve
- Ginger beer, to serve

In a blender, combine the tequila and lime zest. Pulse until the zest is finely chopped but not pureed. Let sit for 3 minutes. Strain through a muslin-lined mesh sieve into a 750-milliliter bottle. Add the crème de cassis and ginger liqueur. Cap the bottle securely, then shake well to mix. Store in the freezer. To serve, pour 3 ounces (90 ml) into a highball glass filled two-thirds with ice cubes. Top with ginger beer.

Thirsty for more?
If you have some blanco tequila to spare, try a:

Tequila Mojito HERBAL | SWEET | SMOKY | SOUR

MAKES 1 COCKTAIL

- 2 sprigs fresh mint
- ½ ounce (15 ml) agave syrup
- 3 ounces (90 ml) blanco tequila
- 1 ounce (30 ml) lime juice
- 6 to 10 granules sea salt
- Ice cubes

In a cocktail shaker, muddle 1 sprig of mint and the syrup, then leave the muddler in the shaker. Add the tequila, lime juice and salt, then swish the muddler to rinse it. Shake with ice cubes, then strain into a highball glass filled halfway with ice cubes. Garnish with the remaining sprig of mint.

La Rosita HERBAL | SWEET | FRUITY

If you love a Negroni, you'll love La Rosita. It takes the three-ingredient classic and swaps the smoky side of tequila in place of the more botanical gin. It's a twist that most people agree was born during the latter half of the 20th century. Credit for popularizing it goes to Gary "Gaz" Regan, who included a version of it in his 1991 *The Bartender's Bible*. I like to take the richness up a bit with a combination of orange and chocolate bitters.

 STARTING WITH A FULL BOTTLE?
Pour off 12 ounces (360 ml).

MAKES 5 TO 7 COCKTAILS

- 13 ounces (390 ml) reposado tequila
- 3½ ounces (105 ml) Campari
- 3½ ounces (105 ml) sweet vermouth
- 3½ ounces (105 ml) dry vermouth
- ¼ teaspoon (2 ml) orange bitters
- ¼ teaspoon (2 ml) chocolate bitters
- Ice cubes, to serve

In a 750-milliliter bottle, combine the tequila, Campari, sweet vermouth, dry vermouth and both bitters. Cap the bottle securely, then shake well to mix. Store in the freezer. To serve, pour into a rocks glass with 1 large or 2 standard ice cubes.

Thirsty for more?
If you have some reposado tequila to spare, try an:

Agave Spritz BITTER | SMOKY | SWEET

MAKES 1 COCKTAIL

- 2 ounces (60 ml) reposado tequila
- 1 ounce (30 ml) Aperol
- Dash orange bitters
- Ice cubes
- 2 ounces (60 ml) sparkling wine
- 1 slice orange

In a wineglass, combine the tequila, Aperol and bitters. Stir. Add enough ice to fill the glass about two-thirds. Top with sparkling wine and add the orange slice.

Little Devil SWEET | SPICY | STRONG

If you like a spicy Margarita, you'll love the Little Devil. There are all manner of cocktails running around with this name. My version spikes blanco tequila with a sweet-and-spicy blend of chili liqueur and cherry brandy. When I serve this, I sometimes dirty it up by adding a dash of pickled jalapeño brine to the glass.

STARTING WITH A FULL BOTTLE?
Pour off 10 ounces (300 ml).

MAKES 5 TO 7 COCKTAILS

- 15 ounces (450 ml) blanco tequila
- 4 ounces (120 ml) Ancho Reyes chili liqueur
- 2 ounces (60 ml) cherry brandy
- 2 ounces (60 ml) agave or simple syrup
- ¼ teaspoon (2 ml) orange bitters
- Generous pinch sea salt
- Crushed ice, to serve

In a 750-milliliter bottle, combine the tequila, Ancho Reyes, brandy, syrup, bitters and salt. Cap the bottle securely, then shake well to mix. Store in the freezer. To serve, pour into a coupe filled halfway with crushed ice.

Thirsty for more?
If you have some blanco tequila to spare, try a:

Guadalajara   CREAMY | SWEET | SPICY | SOUR

MAKES 1 COCKTAIL

- Lime zest strip, 3 inches (8 cm) long
- 1 sprig fresh mint
- ¼ ounce (8 ml) agave syrup
- 2½ ounces (75 ml) blanco tequila
- ½ ounce (15 ml) Ancho Reyes chili liqueur
- Dash chocolate bitters
- Ice cubes

In a cocktail shaker, muddle the lime zest, mint and syrup, then leave the muddler in the shaker. Add the tequila, Ancho Reyes and bitters. Swish the muddler to rinse, then remove. Shake with ice cubes, then double strain into a cocktail glass.

Margarita   SWEET | SOUR | FRUITY | REFRESHING

Jimmy Buffet's liquid dream, right? A full bottle of icy-cold Margaritas at the ready! There is no magic here, just an ample pour (or six) of the tequila love you want and need. I'm a staunch opponent of salted rims; they're too intense and don't allow you to taste anything else in the glass. But I do love a sprinkle of salt in my Margarita. It heightens and brightens every other ingredient.

STARTING WITH A FULL BOTTLE?
Pour off 9 ounces (270 ml).

MAKES 5 TO 7 COCKTAILS

- 16 ounces (480 ml) blanco tequila
- 4 ounces (120 ml) orange liqueur
- 3 ounces (90 ml) lime juice
- 1½ ounces (45 ml) agave or simple syrup
- ¼ teaspoon (6 grams) sea salt
- Ice cubes, to serve

In a 750-milliliter bottle, combine the tequila, orange liqueur, lime juice, syrup and salt. Cap the bottle securely, then shake well to mix. Store in the freezer. To serve, pour into a rocks glass with 1 large or 2 standard ice cubes.

Thirsty for more?
If you have some blanco tequila to spare, try a:

Cabana Boy REFRESHING | CREAMY | SWEET

MAKES 1 COCKTAIL

- 3 ounces (90 ml) blanco tequila
- 1 ounce (30 ml) coconut water
- 1 ounce (30 ml) pineapple juice
- ¼ ounce (8 ml) agave or simple syrup
- Pinch ground cinnamon
- Ice cubes
- Cinnamon stick

In a cocktail shaker, combine the tequila, coconut water, pineapple juice, syrup and ground cinnamon. Shake with ice cubes. Strain into a rocks glass. Garnish with the cinnamon stick.

Mexican Old Fashioned CREAMY | STRONG | SWEET

The original version of this cocktail comes from Limantour in Mexico City, one of the world's best bars. It uses the basic Old Fashioned as a model, but replaces the whiskey with richly aged reposado tequila. The addition of crème de cacao contributes a richness and sweetness that nudge the drink somewhere between Old Fashioned and Manhattan. The orange bitters are my addition, brightening everything and playing so well with the cacao.

STARTING WITH A FULL BOTTLE?
Pour off 5 ounces (150 ml).

MAKES 5 TO 7 COCKTAILS

- 20 ounces (600 ml) reposado tequila
- 4 ounces (120 ml) crème de cacao
- ¼ teaspoon (2 ml) orange bitters
- Ice cubes, to serve

In a 750-milliliter bottle, combine the tequila, crème de cacao and bitters. Cap the bottle securely, then shake well to mix. Store in the freezer. To serve, pour into a rocks glass with 1 large or 2 standard ice cubes.

Thirsty for more?
If you have some reposado tequila to spare, try a:

Guadalajara Dos   HERBAL | SWEET | STRONG

MAKES 1 COCKTAIL

- 2 ounces (60 ml) reposado tequila
- 1 ounce (30 ml) dry vermouth
- ½ ounce (15 ml) Bénédictine
- Ice cubes

In a stirring glass, combine the tequila, vermouth and Bénédictine. Stir with ice cubes, then strain into a cocktail glass.

Naked and Famous SWEET | SOUR | SMOKY

Sweet, sour and a little smoky, the Naked and Famous was created by Joaquín Simó at New York City's Death & Co. His version calls for equal parts of all ingredients, but I prefer to let the mezcal shine a little brighter, so I dial back the Aperol. This cocktail traditionally includes lime juice. To make its transition to the freezer a little smoother, I use just the zest to add bright aromatic notes.

STARTING WITH A FULL BOTTLE?
Pour off 17 ounces (510 ml).

MAKES 5 TO 7 COCKTAILS

- 8 ounces (240 ml) mezcal
- 8 ounces (240 ml) Yellow Chartreuse
- 6 ounces (180 ml) Aperol
- 2 ounces (60 ml) water
- Ice cubes, to serve
- Lime zest strips, to serve

In a 750-milliliter bottle, combine the mezcal, Yellow Chartreuse, Aperol and water. Cap the bottle securely, then shake well to mix. Store in the freezer. To serve, pour into a rocks glass with 1 large or 2 standard ice cubes. Rub a lime zest strip around the rim of the glass, then add it to the drink.

Thirsty for more?
If you have some mezcal to spare, try an:

Agave Fumar SWEET | SMOKY | FRUITY

MAKES 1 COCKTAIL
- 3 ounces (90 ml) mezcal
- ¼ ounce (8 ml) agave syrup
- ¼ ounce (8 ml) lemon juice
- Pinch smoked paprika
- Ice cubes

In a cocktail shaker, combine the mezcal, syrup, lemon juice and paprika. Shake with ice cubes, then strain into a coupe with 1 large ice cube.

Smoked and Sassy   SWEET | CREAMY | SMOKY

This cocktail drinks like a sassy Manhattan. If you prefer something a little less fruity (and a little more Manhattan-y), swap Angostura bitters for the orange. You also can lose the maraschino liqueur and up the sweet vermouth by the same amount.

 **STARTING WITH A FULL BOTTLE?**
Pour off 10 ounces (300 ml).

MAKES 5 TO 7 COCKTAILS

- 15 ounces (450 ml) blanco tequila
- 3½ ounces (105 ml) sweet vermouth
- 3½ ounces (105 ml) maraschino liqueur
- 2 ounces (60 ml) water
- ¼ teaspoon (2 ml) orange bitters
- Ice cubes, to serve

In a 750-milliliter bottle, combine the tequila, sweet vermouth, maraschino liqueur, water and bitters. Cap the bottle securely, then shake well to mix. Store in the freezer. To serve, pour into a rocks glass with 1 large or 2 standard ice cubes.

Thirsty for more?
If you have some blanco tequila to spare, try a:

Santa's Margarita SWEET | CREAMY | STRONG

MAKES 1 COCKTAIL

- 3 ounces (90 ml) blanco tequila
- ½ ounce (15 ml) Licor 43
- ¼ ounce (8 ml) agave or simple syrup
- ¼ ounce (8 ml) lemon juice
- Pinch ground cinnamon
- Pinch nutmeg
- 6 to 10 granules sea salt
- Ice, cubes and crushed

In a cocktail shaker, combine the tequila, Licor 43, syrup, lemon juice, cinnamon, nutmeg and salt. Shake with ice cubes. Strain into a coupe filled halfway with crushed ice.

AGAVE (TEQUILA AND MEZCAL)

Tequila Spritz BITTER | SWEET | STRONG | SMOKY

This cocktail lives in a happy place somewhere between sangria and an Aperol Spritz. It typically isn't topped with bubbles, but I decided to lean into the spritz and top it with tonic water. If you'd prefer it sans bubbles, just serve in a coupe filled halfway with crushed ice, and skip the tonic. Either way, sip in the sun, preferably while lounging by the water.

STARTING WITH A FULL BOTTLE?
Pour off 15 ounces (450 ml).

MAKES 5 TO 7 COCKTAILS

- 10 ounces (300 ml) blanco tequila
- 6¾ ounces (203 ml) Aperol
- 6¾ ounces (203 ml) sweet vermouth
- ¼ teaspoon (2 ml) orange bitters
- Ice cubes, to serve
- Orange slices, to serve
- Tonic water, to serve

In a 750-milliliter bottle, combine the tequila, Aperol, sweet vermouth and bitters. Cap the bottle securely, then shake well to mix. Store in the freezer. To serve, pour into a wine glass filled halfway with ice cubes and an orange slice. Top with tonic water.

Thirsty for more?
If you have some sweet vermouth to spare, try:

The Bitter Spaniard

SWEET | FRUITY | BITTER | REFRESHING | SOUR

MAKES 1 COCKTAIL

- 4 ounces (120 ml) sweet vermouth
- 1 ounce (30 ml) Aperol
- 1 teaspoon (7 grams) raspberry jam
- ¼ ounce (8 ml) lime juice
- Ice cubes
- Orange round

In a cocktail shaker, combine the vermouth, Aperol, jam and lime juice. Shake with ice cubes. Double strain into a rocks glass with 1 large or 2 standard ice cubes. Float the orange round on top.

AGAVE (TEQUILA AND MEZCAL)

Venial Sin   HERBAL | STRONG | SWEET

There's nothing subtle about a Venial Sin. Just the way we want it. Clean, herbal and strong with a pop of spice and smoke—thanks to the blend of reposado tequila and mezcal—this is a great drink that demands your attention. It typically is made with Yellow Chartreuse, but I favor a hit of absinthe. The anise notes of the latter help balance the floral-fruitiness of the maraschino and elderflower liqueurs. The chili bitters add a lovely background of heat. If you don't have chili bitters, a drop of hot sauce stirred in when you serve works fine.

STARTING WITH A FULL BOTTLE?
Pour off 14½ ounces (435 ml).

MAKES 5 TO 7 COCKTAILS

- 10½ ounces (315 ml) reposado tequila
- 3½ ounces (105 ml) mezcal
- 3 ounces (90 ml) water
- 1¾ ounces (53 ml) absinthe
- 1¾ ounces (53 ml) maraschino liqueur
- 1¾ ounces (53 ml) elderflower liqueur
- ¼ teaspoon (2 ml) chili bitters

In a 750-milliliter bottle, combine the tequila, mezcal, water, absinthe, maraschino liqueur, elderflower liqueur and bitters. Cap the bottle securely, then shake well to mix. Store in the freezer. To serve, pour into a cocktail glass.

Thirsty for more?
If you have some reposado tequila to spare, try a:

Roaring '50s   HERBAL | SWEET | STRONG

MAKES 1 COCKTAIL

- 2 ounces (60 ml) reposado tequila
- ½ ounce (15 ml) Cocchi Americano or Lillet Blanc
- ½ ounce (15 ml) Cynar
- ¼ ounce (8 ml) grenadine
- Dash absinthe
- Ice cubes

In a cocktail shaker, combine the tequila, Cocchi Americano or Lillet Blanc, Cynar, grenadine and absinthe. Shake with ice cubes, then strain into a rocks glass with 1 large or 2 standard ice cubes.

AGAVE (TEQUILA AND MEZCAL)

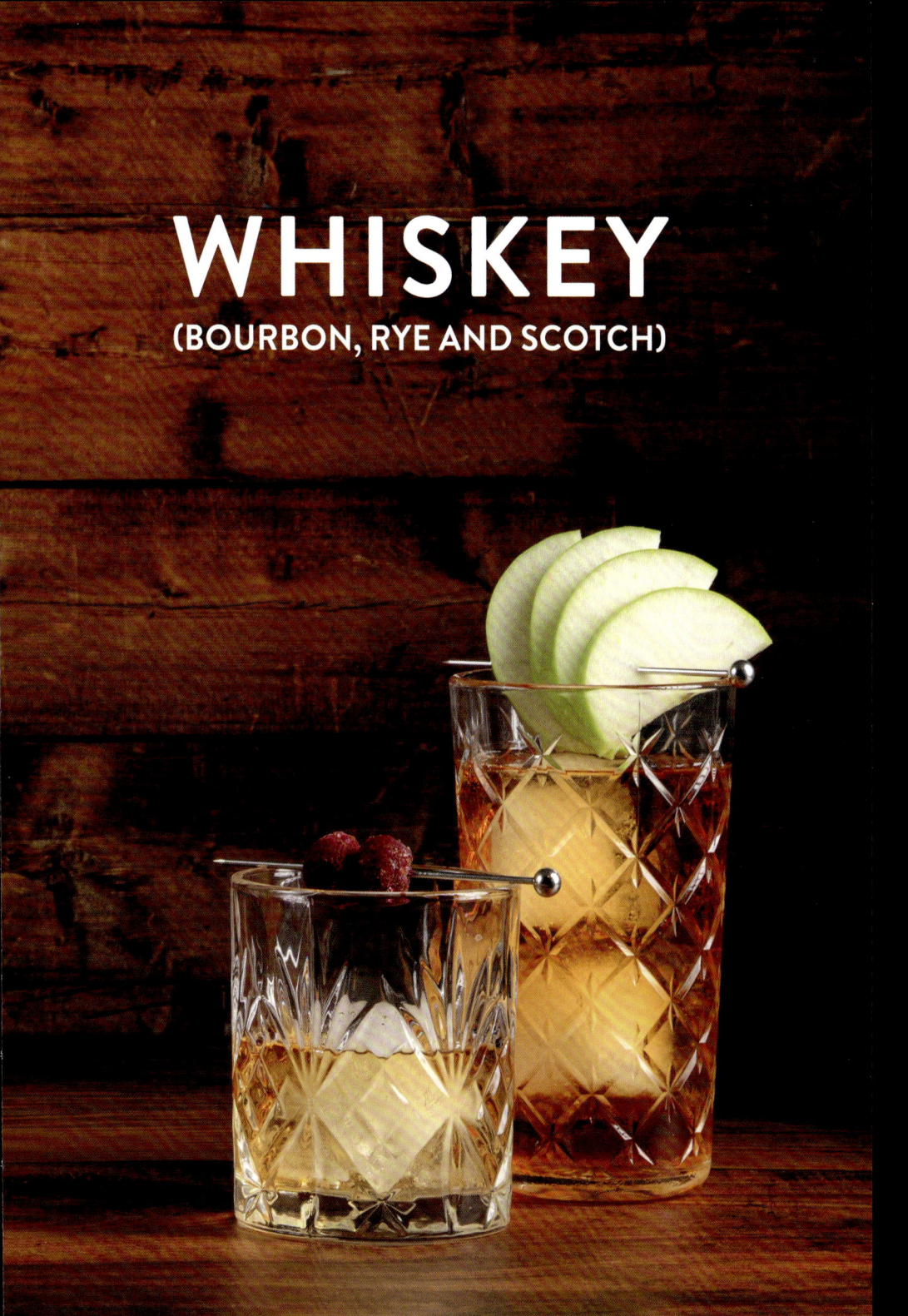

WHISKEY
(BOURBON, RYE AND SCOTCH)

Almond Joy   CREAMY | SWEET | STRONG

This irresistibly creamy-sweet cocktail starts life looking rather disheveled. But like most of us, it eventually pulls itself together and looks pretty dashing in the glass. The issue is the almond butter, which we use to fat-wash the bourbon. It doesn't look all that pretty when you're making it, but once you strain out the almond butter and are left with nutty-rich bourbon, you'll see why it was worth it.

 **STARTING WITH A FULL BOTTLE?**
Pour off 5 ounces (150 ml).

MAKES 5 TO 7 COCKTAILS

2 tablespoons (30 g) almond butter

20 ounces (600 ml) bourbon

2 ounces (60 ml) water

1½ ounces (45 ml) Cynar

1½ ounces (45 ml) agave or simple syrup

¼ teaspoon (2 ml) orange bitters

Ice cubes, to serve

Orange zest twists, to serve

In a heat-proof liquid measuring cup with at least a 4-cup (2-pint or 1-liter) capacity, microwave the almond butter for 30 seconds, or until soft and easily stirred. Mix in the bourbon; it won't be smooth. Let sit at room temperature for 5 minutes, stirring often. Place in the freezer for 45 minutes. Strain through a muslin-lined mesh sieve into a 750-milliliter bottle; discard the solids. Add the water, Cynar, syrup and bitters. Cap the bottle securely, then shake well to mix. Store in the freezer. To serve, pour into a rocks glass with 1 large or 2 standard ice cubes. Garnish with an orange zest twist.

Thirsty for more?
If you have some bourbon to spare, try a:

Bourbon Algonquin FRUITY | STRONG | CREAMY

MAKES 1 COCKTAIL

2 ounces (60 ml) bourbon

1 ounce (30 ml) pineapple juice

½ ounce (15 ml) dry vermouth

¾ teaspoon (4 ml) agave or simple syrup

Dash orange bitters

6 to 10 granules sea salt

Ice cubes

In a cocktail shaker, combine the bourbon, pineapple juice, dry vermouth, syrup, bitters and salt. Shake with ice cubes, then strain into a cocktail glass.

Bacon Old Fashioned SWEET | CREAMY | STRONG

The beauty of this cocktail is that not only do you get a full bottle of amazingly rich, bacon-infused Old Fashioned to sip, you also get a bunch of bacon to eat! Win-win! The technique here is simple: cook bacon until crisp and the fat has rendered. Add that fat to bourbon and let it sit for a bit. This allows the alcohol-soluble flavor molecules in the bacon fat to infuse the bourbon. The bourbon then is chilled to remove the fat, but the flavor stays behind. It's up to you, but I skip smoked bacons; the flavor tends to overwhelm. I like the brightness that orange bitters add, but Angostura also works fine.

 STARTING WITH A FULL BOTTLE?
Pour off 3 ounces (90 ml).
MAKES 5 TO 7 COCKTAILS

- 5 strips thick-cut bacon
- 22 ounces (660 ml) bourbon
- 1½ ounces (45 ml) agave or simple syrup
- ¼ teaspoon (2 ml) orange bitters
- Ice cubes, to serve

In a large frying pan over medium-low heat, cook the bacon until it is crisp and has rendered ¼ cup (2 ounces, 60 ml) or more of fat, about 10 minutes. Use tongs to remove the bacon from the pan, letting any fat drip back into the pan. Eat the bacon or refrigerate for another use. Using a silicone spatula, scrape the bacon fat from the pan into a liquid measuring cup with at least a 4-cup (2-pint or 1-liter) capacity. Add the bourbon and let sit at room temperature, stirring often, for 10 minutes. Place in the freezer for 1 hour; the fat will solidify on top of the bourbon. Strain through a muslin-lined mesh sieve into a 750-milliliter bottle; discard the solids. Add the syrup and bitters to the bottle. Cap the bottle securely, then shake well to mix. Store in the freezer. To serve, pour into a rocks glass with 1 large or 2 standard ice cubes.

Thirsty for more?
If you have some bourbon to spare, try a:

Nutcracker CREAMY | STRONG | FRUITY

MAKES 1 COCKTAIL

- 2½ ounces (75 ml) bourbon
- ½ ounce (15 ml) Frangelico
- ¼ ounce (8 ml) amaretto
- ¼ ounce (8 ml) orgeat syrup
- ¼ ounce (8 ml) lemon juice
- 6 to 10 granules sea salt
- Ice cubes

In a cocktail shaker, combine the bourbon, Frangelico, amaretto, orgeat syrup, lemon juice and salt. Shake with ice cubes, then strain into a coupe.

Blood and Sand STRONG | FRUITY

The Blood and Sand is named after a 1922 movie by the same name. The cocktail later was popularized by Harry Craddock. Classic versions call for scotch, cherry brandy, sweet vermouth and orange juice. That's a lot. I prefer a less chaotic version that ditches the peaty scotch in favor of peppery rye. I also skip the orange juice but retain the citrus brightness by using orange bitters (which also happen to be more freezer friendly).

STARTING WITH A FULL BOTTLE?
Pour off 9 ounces (270 ml).

MAKES 5 TO 7 COCKTAILS

- 16 ounces (480 ml) rye
- 2 ounces (60 ml) water
- 1¾ ounces (53 ml) cherry brandy
- 1¾ ounces (53 ml) sweet vermouth
- 1¾ ounces (53 ml) agave or simple syrup
- ¼ teaspoon (2 ml) orange bitters
- Ice cubes, to serve

In a 750-milliliter bottle, combine the rye, water, cherry brandy, sweet vermouth, syrup and bitters. Cap the bottle securely, then shake well to mix. Store in the freezer. To serve, pour into a rocks glass with 1 large or 2 standard ice cubes.

Thirsty for more?
If you have some rye to spare, try an:

Eau de Tang STRONG | FRUITY | SWEET

MAKES 1 COCKTAIL

- Orange zest strip or coin
- 1 ounce (30 ml) rye
- 1 ounce (30 ml) bourbon
- 1 ounce (30 ml) brandy
- ¼ ounce (8 ml) agave or simple syrup
- Dash orange bitters
- 1 large or 2 standard ice cubes

Rub the zest along the rim of a rocks glass, then add it to the glass. Add the rye, bourbon, brandy, syrup, bitters and ice cubes, then stir.

Bobby Burns STRONG | SWEET | FRUITY

Just as the Rob Roy is a scotch-based relative of the Manhattan, the Bobby Burns uses scotch to create a close cousin of the Vieux Carré. Like the Vieux Carré, the Bobby Burns traditionally is stirred with ice, so we add a little water to the bottle to compensate. Alternatively, you can leave out the water, add an equal amount of scotch, and serve this in a rocks glass with a large ice cube. As for the scotch, opt for something blended, which is just fine for mixing. Also, if you're not a fan of the smoky flavor of peat, consider a low-peat blend; I like Monkey Shoulder.

STARTING WITH A FULL BOTTLE?
Pour off 16 ounces (480 ml).
MAKES 5 TO 7 COCKTAILS

- 9 ounces (270 ml) blended scotch
- 9 ounces (270 ml) sweet vermouth
- 4½ ounces (135 ml) Bénédictine
- 2 ounces (60 ml) water
- Lemon zest strip, to serve

In a 750-milliliter bottle, combine the scotch, sweet vermouth, Bénédictine and water. Cap the bottle securely, then shake well to mix. Store in the freezer. To serve, pour into a coupe. Rub a lemon zest strip around the rim of the glass, then add to the glass.

Thirsty for more?
If you have some scotch to spare, try a:

Tropical Tartan CREAMY | SWEET | STRONG | SMOKY

MAKES 1 COCKTAIL

- 3 ounces (90 ml) blended scotch
- ½ ounce (15 ml) ginger liqueur
- ¼ ounce (8 ml) honey
- Chunk of banana, 2 inches (5 cm) long
- Ice, cubes and crushed

In a cocktail shaker, dry shake the scotch, ginger liqueur and honey (without ice). Add the banana, smashing it as you do so. Shake again with ice cubes. Double strain into a coupe filled halfway with crushed ice.

Boulevardier BITTER | STRONG | SWEET

Another close cousin of the Negroni (see La Rosita on page 106 for a tequila take on this equation), the Boulevardier is a simple blend of bourbon, bittersweet Campari and sweet vermouth. The recipe dates to the 1920s, supposedly created by Erskine Gwynne, an American writer living in Paris who founded a magazine called *Boulevardier*—a term that loosely (and appropriately) translates as "wealthy, fashionable socialite."

STARTING WITH A FULL BOTTLE?
Pour off 9 ounces (270 ml).
MAKES 5 TO 7 COCKTAILS

- 16 ounces (480 ml) bourbon
- 4½ ounces (135 ml) Campari
- 4½ ounces (135 ml) sweet vermouth
- Ice cubes, to serve
- Maraschino cherries, to serve

In a 750-milliliter bottle, combine the bourbon, Campari and sweet vermouth. Cap the bottle securely, then shake well to mix. Store in the freezer. To serve, pour into a rocks glass with 1 large or 2 standard ice cubes. Garnish with a maraschino cherry on a cocktail skewer for stirring.

Thirsty for more?
If you have some bourbon to spare, try:

The Love Bug STRONG | BITTER | SWEET

MAKES 1 COCKTAIL

- 2½ ounces (75 ml) bourbon
- ½ ounce (15 ml) Campari
- ½ ounce (15 ml) Cognac
- Dash Angostura bitters
- Ice cubes

In a cocktail shaker, combine the bourbon, Campari, Cognac and bitters. Shake with ice cubes. Strain into a coupe.

Brooklyn STRONG | HERBAL | SPICY

The challenge of creating a freezer version of the Brooklyn—a bittersweet rye-based cocktail that drinks a bit like a dry Manhattan—was less about preventing it from freezing and more about finding good alternatives to one of the ingredients traditionally called for in the original recipe: Amer Picon, an amaro with orange notes. That's a bit hard to find these days, so I use a blend of Fernet-Branca amaro and orange liqueur. The good news is that both handle the freezer just fine.

 STARTING WITH A FULL BOTTLE?
Pour off 13 ounces (390 ml).

MAKES 5 TO 7 COCKTAILS

12 ounces (360 ml) rye

3 ounces (90 ml) dry vermouth

3 ounces (90 ml) orange liqueur

2 ounces (60 ml) water

1½ ounces (45 ml) Fernet-Branca amaro

1½ ounces (45 ml) maraschino liqueur

Generous pinch sea salt

Ice cubes, to serve

In a 750-milliliter bottle, combine the rye, dry vermouth, orange liqueur, water, Fernet-Branca, maraschino liqueur and salt. Cap the bottle securely, then shake well to mix. Store in the freezer. To serve, pour into a rocks glass with 1 large or 2 standard ice cubes.

Thirsty for more?
If you have some rye to spare, try a:

Sazerac STRONG | HERBAL | SWEET

MAKES 1 COCKTAIL

Splash absinthe

2 ounces (60 ml) rye

½ ounce (15 ml) Cognac

¼ ounce (8 ml) agave or simple syrup

Dash Angostura bitters

Dash Peychaud's bitters

Ice cubes

1 lemon zest strip

Pour the absinthe into a Nick and Nora glass, then swirl to coat the inside. Dump out and discard the absinthe. In a stirring glass, combine the rye, Cognac, syrup and both bitters. Stir with ice cubes, then strain into the glass. Rub the lemon zest strip around the rim of the glass, then express it (squeeze it) over the cocktail and discard.

Dry Manhattan HERBAL | STRONG

For an herbal take on the classic Manhattan, we swap dry vermouth for the more traditional sweet. The resulting cocktail is herbal and strong, a wonderful slow sipper. You don't need to use both Angostura and orange bitters, but they work marvelously together in this cocktail. You also could use chocolate bitters instead of Angostura. A strip of lemon zest is essential for the finished cocktail, so be sure to have some on hand for serving.

STARTING WITH A FULL BOTTLE?
Pour off 7½ ounces (225 ml).

MAKES 5 TO 7 COCKTAILS

- 17½ ounces (525 ml) rye
- 3½ ounces (105 ml) dry vermouth
- 2½ ounces (80 ml) water
- 1 ounce (30 ml) agave or simple syrup
- ¼ teaspoon (2 ml) Angostura bitters
- ¼ teaspoon (2 ml) orange bitters
- Lemon zest strips, to serve
- Ice cubes, to serve
- Maraschino cherries, to serve

In a 750-milliliter bottle, combine the rye, vermouth, water, syrup and both bitters. Cap the bottle securely, then shake well to mix. Store in the freezer. To serve, run a lemon zest strip around the rim of a rocks glass with 1 large or 2 standard ice cubes, then add the zest and a cherry. Pour the cocktail into the glass.

Thirsty for more?
If you have some rye to spare, try a:

Rye San Martin Cocktail

HERBAL | SWEET | STRONG

MAKES 1 COCKTAIL
- 2 ounces (60 ml) rye
- ½ ounce (15 ml) sweet vermouth
- ¼ ounce (8 ml) Green Chartreuse
- Ice cubes

In a stirring glass, combine the rye, sweet vermouth and Green Chartreuse. Stir with ice cubes, then strain into a cocktail glass.

WHISKEY (BOURBON, RYE AND SCOTCH)

Manhattan WARM | STRONG | SWEET | SPICY

The classic Manhattan is a stirred cocktail served neat. To ensure we get the proper level of dilution in the freezer version, we mix it neat, then serve it over ice. After a moment in the glass, you'll hit the perfect mix. I also add a bit of maraschino cherry syrup (from the cherry jar). That ensures the cherry sweetness is evenly mixed into the cocktail even before you pour it. But be sure to use high-quality candied cherries, such as Luxardo. Save those fluorescent cherries sold in most supermarkets for ice cream sundaes. While rye is the traditional choice, I'm also happy with a bourbon version; mix as you see fit.

STARTING WITH A FULL BOTTLE?
Pour off 5 ounces (150 ml).
MAKES 5 TO 7 COCKTAILS

WHISKEY (BOURBON, RYE AND SCOTCH)

- 20 ounces (600 ml) rye or bourbon
- 4 ounces (120 ml) sweet vermouth
- ½ ounce (15 ml) maraschino cherry syrup
- ¼ teaspoon (2 ml) Angostura bitters
- Maraschino cherries, to serve
- Ice cubes, to serve

In a 750-milliliter bottle, combine the rye or bourbon, sweet vermouth, syrup and bitters. Cap the bottle securely, then shake to mix. Store in the freezer. To serve, pour into a rocks glass with 1 cherry and 1 large or 2 standard ice cubes.

Thirsty for more?
If you have some rye or bourbon to spare, try a:

Dolce Vita CREAMY | STRONG | SWEET

MAKES 1 COCKTAIL

- 2 ounces (60 ml) rye or bourbon
- ½ ounce (15 ml) sweet vermouth
- ¼ ounce (8 ml) Frangelico
- ¾ teaspoon (4 ml) agave or simple syrup
- Dash orange bitters
- Ice cubes

In a stirring glass, combine the rye or bourbon, sweet vermouth, Frangelico, syrup and bitters. Stir with ice cubes. Strain into a cocktail glass.

WHISKEY (BOURBON, RYE AND SCOTCH)

Mint Julep STRONG | SWEET | HERBAL | REFRESHING

Though made famous by the Kentucky Derby, the Mint Julep actually predates it by a long while. This mint-spiked bourbon cocktail, which has been sipped for a good 200 or more years, is one of an entire class of cocktails called juleps (basically any liquor poured over crushed ice). Adapting it to the freezer was tricky. Fresh mint is a key ingredient, and it's not a fan of being frozen. My solution was to create a simple syrup infused with fresh mint. Add that to a bottle of bourbon, and you are ready for the races!

 STARTING WITH A FULL BOTTLE?
Pour off 4 ounces (120 ml).

MAKES 5 TO 7 COCKTAILS

- 4 cups (130 g) fresh mint, roughly chopped, plus more sprigs to serve
- ½ cup (100 g) white sugar
- 2 ounces (60 ml) water
- 21 ounces (630 ml) bourbon
- Crushed ice, to serve
- Angostura bitters, to serve

In a medium saucepan over medium heat, combine the mint, sugar and water. Stir, pressing on the mint, until the sugar melts and the mint wilts. Set aside until cool. Once cool, strain through a mesh sieve into a liquid measuring cup. In a 750-milliliter bottle, combine the bourbon and 3½ ounces (105 ml) of the mint syrup. Cap the bottle securely, then shake to mix. Store in the freezer. To serve, fill a rocks glass with crushed ice, then pour in the cocktail. Garnish with several drops of bitters and fresh mint sprigs.

Thirsty for more?
If you have some bourbon to spare, try a:

Bourbon Mojito STRONG | HERBAL | SWEET

MAKES 1 COCKTAIL

- 2 sprigs fresh mint
- 2 lime zest strips
- ½ ounce (15 ml) agave or simple syrup
- 3 ounces (90 ml) bourbon
- Ice cubes
- 2 ounces (60 ml) tonic water

In a cocktail shaker, muddle 1 mint sprig, 1 lime zest strip and the syrup, then leave the muddler in the shaker. Add the bourbon, then swish the muddler to rinse it. Remove the muddler. Shake with ice, then strain into a rocks glass with 1 large or 2 to 3 standard ice cubes. Top with the tonic water. Garnish with the remaining mint sprig and lime zest strip.

Monte Carlo STRONG | HERBAL | CREAMY

The freezer is going upmarket, Old Fashioned style. The Monte Carlo drinks like a sophisticated Old Fashioned thanks to Bénédictine replacing the sugar. It's a French liqueur that is strong, rich and a little sweet and herbal. Original recipes call for serving the Monte Carlo in a cocktail glass. But the freezer version benefits from a little ice, so go for a rocks glass instead.

STARTING WITH A FULL BOTTLE?
Pour off 7½ ounces (225 ml).
MAKES 5 TO 7 COCKTAILS

- 17½ ounces (525 ml) rye
- 3½ ounces (105 ml) Bénédictine
- 3 ounces (90 ml) water
- ¼ teaspoon (2 ml) Angostura bitters
- Pinch sea salt
- Ice cubes, to serve
- Lemon zest twists, to serve

In a 750-milliliter bottle, combine the rye, Bénédictine, water, bitters and salt. Cap the bottle securely, then shake well to mix. Store in the freezer. To serve, pour into a rocks glass with 1 large or 2 standard ice cubes. Garnish with a lemon zest twist.

Thirsty for more?
If you have some rye to spare, try a:

Southern (Hemisphere) Comfort STRONG | HERBAL | CREAMY

MAKES 1 COCKTAIL

- 2 ounces (60 ml) rye
- ½ ounce (15 ml) apricot brandy
- Dash Fernet-Branca amaro
- 6 to 10 granules sea salt
- Ice cubes

In a cocktail shaker, combine the rye, apricot brandy, amaro and salt. Shake with ice cubes, then strain into a coupe.

WHISKEY (BOURBON, RYE AND SCOTCH)

Old Fashioned   STRONG | WARM | SWEET | SPICY | FRUITY

The Old Fashioned is the most classic of classic cocktails, and it lends itself wonderfully to the freezer. A true Old Fashioned should be little more than bourbon or rye, a hint of sugar, a dash of bitters and a smattering of ice. For this freezer version, assemble as you see fit. Use bourbon or rye (bourbon being sweeter, rye being more peppery) and the flavor of bitters that you prefer (orange or Angostura are solid choices, but you do you). I'm a firm believer that ice is the enemy of a good Old Fashioned (I never use more than one small cube), but since this drink is prepared in the bottle and served over ice in the glass, it's easy to adjust to your preferences.

 **STARTING WITH A FULL BOTTLE?**
Pour off 2 ounces (60 ml).

MAKES 5 TO 7 COCKTAILS

- 23 ounces (690 ml) bourbon or rye
- 1 ounce (30 ml) agave or simple syrup
- ¼ teaspoon (2 ml) cocktail bitters (such as orange or Angostura)
- Ice cubes, to serve

In a 750-milliliter bottle, combine the bourbon or rye, syrup and bitters. Cap the bottle securely, then shake to mix. Store in the freezer. To serve, pour into a rocks glass with 1 large or 2 standard ice cubes.

Thirsty for more?
If you have some bourbon or rye to spare, try a:

Dr. B FRUITY | SWEET | STRONG

MAKES 1 COCKTAIL

- 2 ounces (60 ml) bourbon or rye
- ¼ ounce (8 ml) sweet vermouth
- ¼ ounce (8 ml) orange liqueur
- ¾ teaspoon (4 ml) agave or simple syrup
- ¾ teaspoon (4 ml) lime juice
- 6 to 10 granules sea salt
- Ice cubes

In a stirring glass, combine the bourbon or rye, sweet vermouth, orange liqueur, syrup, lime juice and salt. Stir with ice cubes, then strain into a Nick and Nora glass.

WHISKEY (BOURBON, RYE AND SCOTCH)

Paper Plane   STRONG | BITTER | SWEET

The Paper Plane has been around for less than 20 years but already feels like a classic. Credit for the original goes to Sam Ross of Attaboy in New York City. It's a lovely blend of sweet, bitter, herbal and citrus. Tradition calls for equal parts bourbon, Aperol, amaro and lemon juice. I've never been a fan of a strong lemon presence in bourbon cocktails, so I skip the juice in favor of lemon zest in the glass. It's an easy way to get a bright citrus flavor without the acidity that can so easily overwhelm the gentle sweetness of bourbon.

 **STARTING WITH A FULL BOTTLE?**
Pour off 16 ounces (480 ml).

MAKES 5 TO 7 COCKTAILS

- 9 ounces (270 ml) bourbon
- 6 ounces (180 ml) Aperol
- 6 ounces (180 ml) Fernet-Branca amaro
- 3 ounces (90 ml) water
- Ice cubes, to serve
- Lemon zest strips, to serve

In a 750-milliliter bottle, combine the bourbon, Aperol, Fernet-Branca and water. Cap the bottle securely, then shake well to mix. Store in the freezer. To serve, pour into a rocks glass with 1 large or 2 standard ice cubes. Rub a lemon zest strip around the rim, then add to the glass.

Thirsty for more?
If you have some bourbon to spare, try a:

Whiskey Sour STRONG | SWEET | FRUITY

MAKES 1 COCKTAIL

- 1 lemon zest strip
- 2½ ounces (75 ml) bourbon
- ¼ ounce (8 ml) agave or simple syrup
- Dash lemon juice
- 6 to 10 granules sea salt
- Ice cubes

Rub the lemon zest strip around the rim of a rocks glass, then add it to the glass. In a cocktail shaker, combine the bourbon, syrup, lemon juice and salt. Shake with ice cubes. Add 1 large or 2 standard ice cubes to the rocks glass, then strain the cocktail into it.

Philly Assault STRONG | SWEET | SMOKY | BITTER

The Philly Assault is a Manhattan-like cocktail inspired by a drink at the Ranstead Room in Philadelphia. Bénédictine stands in for the sweet vermouth of a Manhattan, while the Cynar sweetens and adds a pleasant bitterness. The result is unexpectedly rich and smooth. Since this cocktail is built in the glass and served on ice, it adapts perfectly to the freezer.

 **STARTING WITH A FULL BOTTLE?**
Pour off 9 ounces (270 ml).

MAKES 5 TO 7 COCKTAILS

16 ounces (480 ml) rye

4 ounces (120 ml) Bénédictine

4 ounces (120 ml) Cynar

¼ teaspoon (2 ml) orange bitters

Ice cubes, to serve

In a 750-milliliter bottle, combine the rye, Bénédictine, Cynar and bitters. Cap the bottle securely, then shake well to mix. Store in the freezer. To serve, pour into a rocks glass with 1 large or 2 standard ice cubes.

Thirsty for more?
If you have some rye to spare, try a:

Luxardo Old Fashioned

STRONG | SWEET | WARM | FRUITY

MAKES 1 COCKTAIL

3 ounces (90 ml) rye

1 maraschino cherry

½ teaspoon syrup from the jar of maraschino cherries

Dash orange bitters

1 large ice cube

In a rocks glass, stir the rye, cherry, syrup, bitters and ice cube.

Pumpkin Spice Martini STRONG | SWEET | CREAMY | SPICY

Why should espresso have all the fun? This simple take on the flavored Martini is such an easy sipper, you'll be glad—and probably hate me a little—when you have a full bottle in your freezer. Be sure to use fresh apple juice to top off this cocktail when serving. Cider won't provide the same sweet, intense autumnal flavor. Feel free to up the flavoring by adding two pinches of pumpkin pie spice. But prep the entire recipe with one pinch, give it a taste, then decide if you want more. A little goes a long way.

STARTING WITH A FULL BOTTLE?
Pour off 6 ounces (180 ml).

MAKES 5 TO 7 COCKTAILS

- 19 ounces (570 ml) bourbon
- 2 ounces (60 ml) agave or simple syrup
- 2 ounces (60 ml) water
- Pinch pumpkin pie spice or ground mixed spice
- ¼ teaspoon (2 ml) orange bitters
- ¼ teaspoon (2 ml) chocolate bitters
- Fresh apple juice, to serve

In a 750-milliliter bottle, combine the bourbon, syrup, water, pumpkin pie spice or ground mixed spice, orange bitters and chocolate bitters. Cap the bottle securely, then shake well to mix. Store in the freezer. To serve, shake, then pour into a cocktail glass, filling it two-thirds of the way. Top with 1 to 2 ounces (30 to 60 ml) fresh apple juice, to taste.

Thirsty for more?
If you have some bourbon to spare, try a:

Vanilla Love CREAMY | SWEET

MAKES 1 COCKTAIL

- 2½ ounces (75 ml) bourbon
- 1 ounce (30 ml) Licor 43
- ½ ounce (15 ml) egg white
- Dash Angostura bitters
- Ice cubes

In a cocktail shaker, combine the bourbon, Licor 43, egg white and bitters. Shake with ice cubes. Strain into a coupe.

Rob Roy SMOKY | SWEET | HERBAL

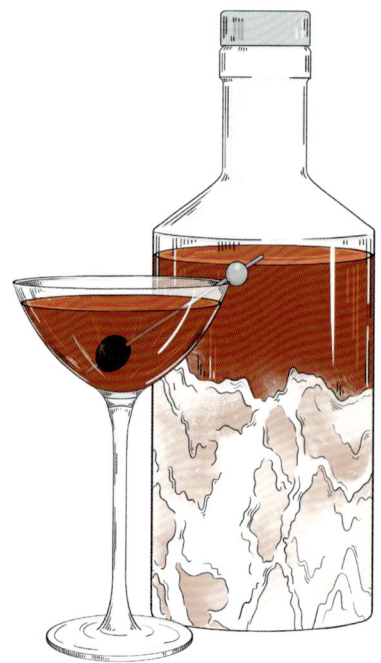

The Rob Roy is scotch's answer to the Manhattan, right down to the maraschino cherry garnish. The result is a lightly smoky, gently sweet cool-weather sipper. The key, of course, is picking the right scotch. Blended is the way to go. After that, decide how much peat (scotch's trademark smoky, earthy flavor) you want. I generally opt for less; my brand is Monkey Shoulder. But go with whatever you prefer.

 STARTING WITH A FULL BOTTLE?
Pour off 7 ounces (210 ml).

MAKES 5 TO 7 COCKTAILS

- 18 ounces (540 ml) blended scotch
- 4½ ounces (135 ml) sweet vermouth
- 2 ounces (60 ml) water
- ¼ teaspoon (2 ml) Angostura bitters
- Maraschino cherries, to serve

In a 750-milliliter bottle, combine the scotch, sweet vermouth, water and bitters. Cap the bottle securely, then shake well to mix. Store in the freezer. To serve, pour into a coupe. Place a cherry on a cocktail skewer and use to stir the cocktail as you sip.

Thirsty for more?
If you have some scotch to spare, try:

The Southie SMOKY | SWEET | BITTER

MAKES 1 COCKTAIL

- 1 ounce (30 ml) blended scotch
- 1 ounce (30 ml) sweet vermouth
- 1 ounce (30 ml) Campari
- Dash orange bitters
- Ice cubes

In a rocks glass, combine the scotch, sweet vermouth, Campari and bitters. Stir with 1 large or 2 standard ice cubes.

Sazerac STRONG | HERBAL | SWEET

The Sazerac has a muddled history, to say the least. For our purposes, we'll satisfy ourselves with the knowledge that it's a strong, herbal and sweet classic that dates to the 1800s in New Orleans. And it lends itself wonderfully to the freezer. My version follows Dale DeGroff's lead and calls for both Angostura and Peychaud's bitters. I like the floral-herbal complexity the combination offers to a drink already firmly in that flavor profile.

STARTING WITH A FULL BOTTLE?
Pour off 9 ounces (270 ml).

MAKES 5 TO 7 COCKTAILS

- 16 ounces (480 ml) rye
- 4 ounces (120 ml) Cognac
- 2 ounces (60 ml) water
- 2 ounces (60 ml) agave or simple syrup
- 1 teaspoon (5 ml) absinthe
- ¼ teaspoon (2 ml) Angostura bitters
- ¼ teaspoon (2 ml) Peychaud's bitters
- Lemon zest strips, to serve

In a 750-milliliter bottle, combine the rye, Cognac, water, syrup, absinthe and both bitters. Cap the bottle securely, then shake well to mix. Store in the freezer. To serve, rub a lemon zest strip around the rim of a Nick and Nora glass. Discard the lemon zest strip, then pour the cocktail into the glass.

Thirsty for more?
If you have some rye to spare, try an:

Improved Whiskey Cocktail

STRONG | HERBAL | FRUITY

MAKES 1 COCKTAIL

- 1 lemon zest strip
- 2½ ounces (75 ml) rye
- ¼ ounce (8 ml) maraschino liqueur
- Dash absinthe
- Dash Angostura bitters
- Dash orange bitters
- Ice cubes

Rub the lemon zest strip around the rim of a cocktail glass, then add it to the glass. In a stirring glass, combine the rye, maraschino liqueur, absinthe, and both bitters. Stir with ice cubes, then strain into the glass.

Sugar Daddy STRONG | SWEET

On paper, the Sugar Daddy looks like a hot mess, with Kahlúa, sweet vermouth and scotch making an unlikely trio. But stay with me. This crazy blend produces a cocktail that is comfortingly sweet and rich. And let's face it, that's kind of the point of a sugar daddy, right? A low-peat blended scotch is the best choice to play well with the richness of the Kahlúa.

STARTING WITH A FULL BOTTLE?
Pour off 7 ounces (210 ml).

MAKES 5 TO 7 COCKTAILS

- 18 ounces (540 ml) blended scotch
- 3 ounces (90 ml) Kahlúa
- 2 ounces (60 ml) water
- 1 ounce (30 ml) sweet vermouth
- ¼ teaspoon (2 ml) Angostura bitters
- Ice cubes, to serve

In a 750-milliliter bottle, combine the scotch, Kahlúa, water, sweet vermouth and bitters. Cap the bottle securely, then shake well to mix. Store in the freezer. To serve, pour into a rocks glass with 1 large or 2 standard ice cubes.

Thirsty for more?
If you have some scotch to spare, try a:

Highland Negroni STRONG | SMOKY | SWEET

MAKES 1 COCKTAIL

- 2½ ounces (75 ml) blended scotch
- 1 ounce (30 ml) sweet vermouth
- ½ ounce (15 ml) Campari
- 1 large or 2 standard ice cubes

In a rocks glass, stir the scotch, vermouth, Campari and ice cubes.

WHISKEY (BOURBON, RYE AND SCOTCH)

Upper East Side STRONG | SWEET | SPICY | BITTER

The Upper East Side is much like a Manhattan, but it has a heck of a lot more going on under the hood (or, in this case, in the freezer). We start with the basic rye and sweet vermouth equation, then add bittersweet Cynar and a bit of peppery ginger liqueur. No cocktail bitters needed for this cozy sipper.

STARTING WITH A FULL BOTTLE?
Pour off 10 ounces (300 ml).

MAKES 5 TO 7 COCKTAILS

15 ounces (450 ml) rye

3½ ounces (105 ml) sweet vermouth

3½ ounces (105 ml) ginger liqueur

2 ounces (60 ml) Cynar

Pinch sea salt

Ice cubes, to serve

In a 750-milliliter bottle, combine the rye, sweet vermouth, ginger liqueur, Cynar and salt. Cap the bottle securely, then shake well to mix. Store in the freezer. To serve, pour into a rocks glass with 1 or 2 large, or 3 to 4 standard ice cubes.

Thirsty for more?
If you have some rye to spare, try:

The Ginger Bear SPICY | STRONG | SWEET

MAKES 1 COCKTAIL

3 ounces (90 ml) rye

3 ounces (90 ml) ginger beer

Dash orange bitters

Ice cubes

In a rocks glass, stir the rye, ginger beer and bitters with 1 large or 2 standard ice cubes.

BRANDY, COGNAC AND VERMOUTH

Americano   BITTER | SWEET | HERBAL | STRONG

The Americano dates back to Milan during the 1860s, but it had to wait nearly 100 years to truly hit pop culture. That's when James Bond ordered it in *Casino Royale*, Ian Fleming's first Bond novel. It's an easy-drinking blend of equal parts Campari—a bittersweet cousin of Aperol—and sweet vermouth poured over ice and topped with carbonated water. I love this style of freezer cocktail because we can batch up a bottle that just needs a few easy steps to serve.

STARTING WITH A FULL BOTTLE?
Pour off 12½ ounces (375 ml).

MAKES 6 COCKTAILS

- 12½ ounces (375 ml) Campari
- 12½ ounces (375 ml) sweet vermouth
- Ice cubes, to serve
- Carbonated water, to serve
- Lemon zest strips, to serve

In a 750-milliliter bottle, combine the Campari and sweet vermouth. Cap the bottle securely, then shake well to mix. Store in the freezer. To serve, fill a highball glass two-thirds with ice, then add 4 ounces (120 ml) of the cocktail mixture and 3 ounces (90 ml) carbonated water. Stir gently. Rub a lemon zest strip around the rim of the glass and add to the glass.

Thirsty for more?
If you have some Campari to spare, try:

The Red Devil FRUITY | BITTER

MAKES 1 COCKTAIL

- 2½ ounces (75 ml) blanco tequila
- 1 ounce (30 ml) mango juice
- ½ ounce (15 ml) Campari
- ¼ ounce (8 ml) agave or simple syrup
- Dash Angostura bitters
- 6 to 10 granules sea salt
- Ice, cubes and crushed

In a cocktail shaker, combine the tequila, juice, Campari, syrup, bitters and salt. Shake with ice cubes, then strain into a coupe filled halfway with crushed ice.

Bosom Caresser STRONG | SWEET | FRUITY

I don't care what you put in this cocktail. With a name like Bosom Caresser, I'm going to drink it. Luckily, if you're hankering for something sweet and easy to drink with some creamy-nutty notes, the Bosom Caresser (I just want to keep saying that) happens to deliver a fine cocktail. The name actually dates to at least the 1930s, but back then it was a different beast, combining mostly fruit, sugar and Curaçao. By a few decades later, it had morphed into this blend of brandy, Madeira and orange liqueur. Since this recipe calls for equal parts of two liquors, consider building it in an empty bottle.

 STARTING WITH A FULL BOTTLE?
Pour off 17 ounces (510 ml).
MAKES 5 TO 7 COCKTAILS

- 8 ounces (240 ml) Madeira
- 8 ounces (240 ml) brandy
- 4 ounces (120 ml) orange liqueur
- 3 ounces (90 ml) water
- Pinch sea salt

In a 750-milliliter bottle, combine the Madeira, brandy, orange liqueur, water and salt. Cap the bottle securely, then shake well to mix. Store in the freezer. To serve, pour into a cocktail glass.

Thirsty for more?
If you have some brandy to spare, try a:

Biting Brandy SWEET | SPICY | FRUITY | STRONG

MAKES 1 COCKTAIL
- 1½ ounces (45 ml) brandy
- 1½ ounces (45 ml) sweet vermouth
- ½ ounce (15 ml) orange liqueur
- ¾ teaspoon (4 ml) cider vinegar
- Ice, cubes and crushed

In a cocktail shaker, combine the brandy, vermouth, orange liqueur and vinegar. Shake with ice cubes. Strain into a coupe filled halfway with crushed ice.

Corpse Reviver No. 1 SWEET | FRUITY | HERBAL | STRONG

Brandy, apple and sweet vermouth? Yes, please! Though it is historically prescribed as a way to ward off the effects of a bad night, this is the perfect winter sipper, and it adapts well to the freezer. The Corpse Reviver No. 2 is more common but shares pretty much nothing with the No. 1, which dates back to Harry Craddock at the Savoy in London. This version is sweet and potent and a little fruity. Not sure it would be my choice for a hair of the dog, but it's a fine cocktail after noon! Since this recipe calls for equal parts Calvados and brandy, consider building it in an empty bottle.

STARTING WITH A FULL BOTTLE?
Pour off 16 ounces (480 ml).

MAKES 5 TO 7 COCKTAILS

9 ounces (270 ml) Calvados

9 ounces (270 ml) brandy

4½ ounces (135 ml) sweet vermouth

2 ounces (60 ml) water

1 ounce (30 ml) agave or simple syrup

Pinch sea salt

Ice cubes, to serve

In a 750-milliliter bottle, combine the Calvados, brandy, sweet vermouth, water, syrup and salt. Cap the bottle securely, then shake well to mix. Store in the freezer. To serve, pour into a rocks glass with 1 large or 2 standard ice cubes.

Thirsty for more?
If you have some brandy to spare, try:

The Sophisticate

REFRESHING | FRUITY | SWEET | SOUR | STRONG

MAKES 1 COCKTAIL

Lemon zest strip or coin

1 ounce (30 ml) sweet vermouth

1 ounce (30 ml) dry vermouth

1 ounce (30 ml) brandy

Dash Angostura bitters

Ice cubes

Sparkling wine

Rub the lemon zest around the rim of a coupe, then add it to the glass. In a cocktail shaker, combine the sweet and dry vermouths, brandy and bitters. Shake with ice cubes. Strain into the glass. Top with sparkling wine.

Sidecar STRONG | SWEET | FRUITY | SOUR

I know that technically this is a Between the Sheets, which is a classic Sidecar (Cognac, orange liqueur and lemon juice) to which you add a bit of white rum. But this is the Sidecar I drink, so that's what I'm calling it. My ratios differ from tradition, mostly because I just don't like the typical Sidecar. The lemon juice dominates in a not pleasant way. This version tamps down the lemon by using only the zest to speed infuse the liquor. And I like the balancing natural sweetness the rum brings.

 STARTING WITH A FULL BOTTLE?
Pour off 12 ounces (360 ml).
MAKES 5 TO 7 COCKTAILS

13 ounces (390 ml) Cognac

6 ounces (180 ml) white rum

3 ounces (90 ml) orange liqueur

Zest strips from 1 lemon

2 ounces (60 ml) water

Pinch sea salt

Ice cubes, to serve

Orange zest strips, to serve

In a blender, combine the Cognac, rum, orange liqueur, lemon zest strips, water and salt. Pulse until the zest is finely chopped but not pureed. Let sit for 3 minutes. Strain through a muslin-lined mesh sieve into a 750-milliliter bottle. Cap the bottle securely, then shake well to mix. Store in the freezer. To serve, pour into a rocks glass with 1 large or 2 standard ice cubes. Garnish with an orange zest strip.

Thirsty for more?
If you have some Cognac to spare, try a:

Roman Punch

STRONG | SWEET | FRUITY | SOUR

MAKES 1 COCKTAIL

2 ounces (60 ml) aged rum

1 ounce (30 ml) Cognac

1 ounce (30 ml) pulp-free orange juice

½ ounce (15 ml) lime juice

¼ ounce (8 ml) orgeat syrup

6 to 10 granules sea salt

Ice, cubes and crushed

In a cocktail shaker, combine the rum, Cognac, orange juice, lime juice, orgeat syrup and salt. Shake with ice cubes, then strain into a coupe filled halfway with crushed ice.

Vieux Carré STRONG | WARM | SWEET | SPICY

The Vieux Carré holds a special place in my heart. It's my daily drink, all warm and sweet and strong, like a good lover. It drinks like a happy dance between a Manhattan and an Old Fashioned. And since it is 100 percent booze, it's an easy convert to the freezer. If you don't have Peychaud's bitters, orange bitters are a good substitute. Since this recipe calls for near equal parts of four liquors, consider building it in an empty bottle.

STARTING WITH A FULL BOTTLE?
Pour off 19 ounces (570 ml).

MAKES 5 TO 7 COCKTAILS

6 ounces (180 ml) rye

6 ounces (180 ml) sweet vermouth

6 ounces (180 ml) Cognac

4½ ounces (135 ml) Bénédictine

2½ ounces (75 ml) water

¼ teaspoon (2 ml) Angostura bitters

¼ teaspoon (2 ml) Peychaud's bitters

Ice cubes, to serve

In a 750-milliliter bottle, combine the rye, sweet vermouth, Cognac, Bénédictine, water and both bitters. Cap the bottle securely, then shake well to mix. Store in the freezer. To serve, pour into a rocks glass with 1 large or 2 standard ice cubes.

Thirsty for more?
If you have some rye to spare, try a:

Carré Reprise STRONG | FRUITY | SWEET

MAKES 1 COCKTAIL

1 ounce (30 ml) rye

1 ounce (30 ml) Cognac

1 ounce (30 ml) sweet vermouth

¼ ounce (8 ml) elderflower liqueur

¾ teaspoon (4 ml) agave or simple syrup

Dash Angostura bitters

Dash Peychaud's bitters

Ice cubes

In a stirring glass, combine the rye, Cognac, sweet vermouth, elderflower liqueur, syrup, Angostura bitters and Peychaud's bitters. Stir with ice cubes, then strain into a coupe.

ACKNOWLEDGMENTS

It's a notion so ludicrous as to verge on arrogance. To consider yourself capable of giving form and substance to an idea that otherwise exists only in the ether of your consciousness. But that is the writer's folly, foe and friend. And for that reason, books come into being only with the all too often unearned support of so many beyond the author. So for all the support I've received from so many and in so many ways, I am immensely grateful.

David Black and the entire team at the David Black Agency. Your unwavering trust when I drag my feet is infuriating in all the right ways.

Michael Szczerban and the team at Little, Brown. Life too often gives us too many reasons to drink. So glad to have you at my side (ordering another round).

Deborah Broide, my font of public relations brilliance. Thank you for standing by me even when I'm a miserable human.

Lika Kviroikashvili, for bringing yet another of my crazy ideas to life in vivid color. Thank you for having such patience with my can-we-just-add-one-more-ice-cube insanity.

And my husband, Nicholas King, without whom all the many hours floating in the vern wouldn't be nearly as fun. Nor as inebriating or annoyingly inspiring. When this book comes out, maybe instead of dying this time, just stick with a simple "Congratulations." Love you.

DRINKS INDEX

A

Agave Fumar, 115
Agave Spritz, 107
Alaska Cocktail, 64–65
All Jammed Up, 25
Almond Joy, 124–125
Amalfi Lemon Margarita, 102–103
Americano, 162–163
Apple Cream Pie, 43
Apple Pie Cocktail, 42–43
Aviation, 66–67

B

Bacon Old Fashioned, 126–127
Bay Breeze, 21
Bee's Knees, 89
Bijou, 68–69
Biting Brandy, 165
Bitter Bastard, 27
Bitter Blood Martini, 10–11
The Bitter Spaniard, 119
Black (and White) Russian, 12–13
Blood and Sand, 128–129
Bloody Mary, 14–15
Blue Moon Cocktail, 70–71
Bobby Burns, 130–131
Bosom Caresser, 164–165
Boulevardier, 132–133
Bourbon Algonquin, 125
Bourbon Mojito, 141
Brando Russian, 16–17
Brooklyn, 134–135
Buttered Rum, 44–45

C

Cabana Boy, 111
Cancan, 39
Caribbean Christmas, 47
Caribbean Cruise, 18–19
Carré Reprise, 171
Chai Slide, 17
Chocolate Negroni, 72–73
Cinnamon Nut Bread, 46–47
Cinnamon Toast Martini, 74–75
Coconut-Lime Daiquiri, 59
Coconut-Lime Daiquiri Colada, 48–49
Coffee Cargo Cocktail, 23
Corpse Reviver No. 1, 166–167
Cosmopolitan, 20–21

D

Daiquiri, 50–51
Damn-the-Weather Cocktail, 76–77
Dolce Vita, 139
Dr. B, 145
Drain the Swamp, 97
Dry Manhattan, 136–137

E

Eau de Tang, 129
El Diablo, 104–105
Espresso Martini, 22–23
Exposition Cocktail, 99

F

Fog Cutter, 19
French Martini, 24–25
Frothed and Fruity, 49

G

Gin and It, 81
Gin Daisy, 65
Gin Fizz, 75
Gin Martini, 78–79
The Ginger Bear, 159
Ginger Screw, 33
Gingersnap Martini, 26–27
Golden Vesper, 87
Guadalajara, 109
Guadalajara Dos, 113

H

Hanky-Panky, 80–81
Harvey Wallbanger (High-End), 28–29
Highland Negroni, 157
The Horse Thief, 82–83

I

Improved Whiskey Cocktail, 155
Inca, 71
Italian Margarita, 103

K

Kiss in the Dark, 84–85

L

La Rosita, 106–107
The Last Word, 86–87
Lemon Drop, 30–31
Lime Cream Pie, 61
Little Devil, 108–109
Little Miss Sunshine, 37
Long Island Iced Tea, 32–33
The Love Bug, 133

Luxardo Old Fashioned, 149
Lychee-Mint Martini, 69

M
Mai Tai, 52–53
Maiden's Blush, 88–89
Make Your Mark, 91
Manhattan, 138–139
Margarita, 110–111
Martinez, 90–91
Mexican Old Fashioned, 112–113
Mint Fizz, 35
Mint Julep, 110–111
Mojito, 54–55
The Monkey Gland, 85
Monte Carlo, 142–143
Moscow Mule, 34–35
Moscow's Sunny Side, 29
Mr. 404, 11

N
Naked and Famous, 114–115
Navy Grog, 51
Negroni, 92–93
1920 Pick-Me-Up, 79
Nutcracker, 127

O
Old Fashioned, 144–145
Old Pal, 93
Orange Martini, 94–95

P
Paper Plane, 146–147
Parisian Blonde, 45
Pegu Club Cocktail, 67
Pendennis Club, 95
Philly Assault, 148–149
The Poet's Dream, 77
Poker Cocktail, 56–57

Pumpkin Spice Martini, 150–151

R
The Red Devil, 163
Rio Jengibre, 15
Roaring '50s, 121
Rob Roy, 152–153
Roman Punch, 169
Rum Daisy, 58–59
Rum Punch, 53
Rumhattan, 57
Rye San Martin Cocktail, 137

S
Santa's Margarita, 117
Satan's Whiskers, 96–97
Sazerac, 135, 154–155
The Sidearm, 83
Sidecar, 168–169
Smoked and Sassy, 116–117
The Sophisticate, 167
Southern (Hemisphere) Comfort, 143
The Southie, 153
Sugar Daddy, 156–157

T
Tahini Martini, 36–37
Tequila Mojito, 105
Tequila Spritz, 118–119
Tropical Coconut Pie, 60–61
Tropical Tartan, 131

U
Up and at 'Em, 73
Upper East Side, 158–159

V
Vanilla Love, 151
Venial Sin, 120–121
Vesper, 98–99

Vieux Carré, 170–171
Vodka Martini, 38–39
Vodka Special, 31

W
Whiskey Sour, 147
White (and Black) Russian, 12–13
White(-ish) Russian, 13

Z
Zombie, 55

INDEX

A

absinthe
　The Horse Thief, 82–83
　Improved Whiskey
　　Cocktail, 155
　1920 Pick-Me-Up, 79
　Roaring '50s, 121
　Sazerac, 135, 154–155
　Venial Sin, 120–121
　Zombie, 55
agave drinks. *See* Mezcal;
　Tequila
alcohol, freezing
　temperatures and, 1. *See also*
　Freezer cocktails
almond butter
　Almond Joy, 124–125
amaretto
　Nutcracker, 127
amaro. *See* Fernet-Branca
　amaro
Ancho Reyes
　All Jammed Up, 25
　Guadalajara, 109
　Little Devil, 108–109
Aperol
　Agave Spritz, 107
　Bitter Bastard, 27
　The Bitter Spaniard,
　　119
　Mr. 404, 11
　Naked and Famous,
　　114–115
　Old Pal, 93
　Paper Plane, 146–147
　Tequila Spritz, 118–119
apple juice
　Apple Cream Pie, 43

Pumpkin Spice Martini,
　150–151
apricot brandy
　Apple Pie Cocktail,
　　42–43
　Pendennis Club, 95
　Southern (Hemisphere)
　　Comfort, 143

B

Bacon Old Fashioned,
　126–127
bananas
　Tropical Tartan, 131
Bénédictine
　Aviation, 66–67
　Bobby Burns, 130–131
　Guadalajara Dos, 113
　Monte Carlo, 142–143
　Philly Assault, 148–149
　The Poet's Dream, 77
　Vieux Carré, 170–171
blender, 6
Blue Curaçao
　Blue Moon Cocktail,
　　70–71
bottles, 5
bourbon. *See* Whiskey
　(bourbon)
brandy. *See also* Apricot
　Brandy; Cherry brandy
　Biting Brandy, 165
　Bosom Caresser, 164–165
　Corpse Reviver No. 1,
　　166–167
　Eau de Tang, 129
　The Sidearm, 83
　The Sophisticate, 167

C

Calvados
　Corpse Reviver No. 1,
　　166–167
Campari
　Americano, 162–163
　Bitter Blood Martini,
　　10–11
　Boulevardier, 132–133
　Chocolate Negroni,
　　72–73
　Highland Negroni, 157
　La Rosita, 106–107
　The Love Bug, 133
　Negroni, 92–93
　The Red Devil, 163
　Rum Punch, 53
　The Southie, 153
Chambord
　French Martini,
　　24–25
Chartreuse. *See* Green
　Chartreuse; Yellow
　Chartreuse
cherry brandy
　Blood and Sand,
　　128–129
　Exposition Cocktail, 99
　Kiss in the Dark, 84–85
　Little Devil, 108–109
cidar
　Buttered Rum, 44–45
cinnamon
　Cabana Boy, 111
　Caribbean Christmas,
　　47
　Cinnamon Nut Bread,
　　46–47

INDEX　　175

cinnamon (*continued*)
    Cinnamon Toast Martini, 74–75
    Santa's Margarita, 112
    Zombie, 55
Cocchi Americano
    Exposition Cocktail, 99
    Vesper, 98–99
cocktails. *See* Freezer cocktails; *specific ingredients*
cocoa powder
    Chai Slide, 17
coconut milk
    Coconut-Lime Daiquiri, 59
coconut water
    Cabana Boy, 111
    Caribbean Christmas, 47
    Frothed and Fruity, 49
    Italian Margarita, 103
    Lime Cream Pie, 61
    Tropical Coconut Pie, 60–61
    White(-ish) Russian, 13
coffee. *See* Espresso
Cognac
    Carré Reprise, 171
    Fog Cutter, 18–19
    The Love Bug, 133
    Roman Punch, 169
    Sazerac, 135, 154–155
    Sidecar, 168–169
    Vieux Carré, 170–171
cranberry juice
    Bay Breeze, 21
    Cosmopolitan, 20–21
cream
    Parisian Blonde, 45
crème de cacao
    Chocolate Negroni, 72–73
    Mexican Old Fashioned, 112–113

crème de cassis
    El Diablo, 104–105
crème de violette
    Blue Moon Cocktail, 70–71
Cynar
    Almond Joy, 124–125
    Philly Assault, 148–149
    Roaring '50s, 121
    Upper East Side, 158–159

D

Daiquiri
    Coconut-Lime Daiquiri, 59
    Coconut-Lime Daiquiri Colada, 48–49
diluting cocktails, 2
dry vermouth. *See* Vermouth, dry

E

egg white
    Apple Cream Pie, 43
    Caribbean Christmas, 47
    Frothed and Fruity, 49
    Gin Fizz, 75
    Vanilla Love, 151
elderflower liqueur
    Carré Reprise, 171
    Mr. 404, 11
    Old Pal, 93
    Venial Sin, 120–121
equipment, essential, 5–7
espresso
    Espresso Martini, 11–13
espresso Martini
    Coffee Cargo Cocktail, 23

F

falernum syrup
    Zombie, 55
fat-washing, 3

fennel seeds
    The Monkey Gland, 85
Fernet-Branca amaro
    Brooklyn, 134–135
    Hanky-Panky, 80–81
    Paper Plane, 146–147
    Southern (Hemisphere) Comfort, 143
Frangelico
    Bacon Old Fashioned, 126–127
    Dolce Vita, 138–139
freezer cocktails
    about, vi–vii
    alcohol, freezing temperatures and, 1
    bottles for, 5
    characteristics of, vii
    diluting with water, 2
    essential gear, 5–7
    fat-washing, 3
    freezing, 2
    ice for, 6–7
    science of, 1–3
    skipping freezing, 3
    splash on top of, 3
    temperature for serving, 2–3
    thawing frozen cocktails, 2
    tricks to making, vi–vii
    what they are, vi

G

Galliano
    Harvey Wallbanger (High-End), 28–29
gear, essential, 5–7
gin
    Alaska Cocktail, 64–65
    Aviation, 66–67

Bee's Knees, 89
Bijou, 68–69
Blue Moon Cocktail, 70–71
Chocolate Negroni, 72–73
Cinnamon Toast Martini, 74–75
Damn-the-Weather Cocktail, 76–77
Drain the Swamp, 97
Exposition Cocktail, 99
Fog Cutter, 19
Gin and It, 81
Gin Daisy, 65
Gin Fizz, 75
Gin Martini, 78–79
Golden Vesper, 87
Hanky-Panky, 80–81
The Horse Thief, 82–83
Inca, 71
Kiss in the Dark, 84–85
The Last Word, 86–87
Long Island Iced Tea, 32–33
Lychee-Mint Martini, 69
Maiden's Blush, 88–89
Make Your Mark, 91
Martinez, 90–91
The Monkey Gland, 85
Negroni, 92–93
1920 Pick-Me-Up, 79
Old Pal, 93
Orange Martini, 94–95
Pegu Club Cocktail, 67
Pendennis Club, 95
The Poet's Dream, 77
Satan's Whiskers, 96–97
The Sidearm, 83
Up and at 'Em, 73
Vesper, 98–99

ginger
    Gingersnap Martini, 26–27
    Moscow Mule, 34–35
    Rio Jengibre, 15
ginger beer
    El Diablo, 104–105
    The Ginger Bear, 159
ginger liqueur
    Bee's Knees, 89
    El Diablo, 104–105
    Ginger Screw, 33
    Gingersnap Martini, 26–27
    Tropical Tartan, 131
    Upper East Side, 158–159
grapefruit juice
    Bitter Bastard, 27
    Drain the Swamp, 97
    Navy Grog, 51
    Old Pal, 93
Green Chartreuse
    Bijou, 68–69
    The Last Word, 86–87
    Rye San Martin Cocktail, 137
grenadine
    Apple Pie Cocktail, 42–43
    Caribbean Cruise, 18–19
    Gin Daisy, 65
    Maiden's Blush, 88–89
    The Monkey Gland, 85
    Roaring '50s, 121
    Zombie, 55

H
honey
    Bee's Knees, 69
    Navy Grog, 51
    Tropical Tartan, 131

I
ice, 6–7
ice cream
    Coffee Cargo Cocktail, 23

J
jiggers, 7

K
Kahlúa
    Black (and White) Russian, 12–13
    Brando Russian, 16–17
    Coffee Cargo Cocktail, 23
    Espresso Martini, 22–23
    Sugar Daddy, 157
    White(-ish) Russian, 19

L
lemon juice
    Agave Fumar, 115
    Bee's Knees, 89
    Bloody Mary, 14–15
    Gin Daisy, 65
    Gin Fizz, 75
    Gingersnap Martini, 26–27
    Lemon Drop, 30–31
    Long Island Iced Tea, 32–33
    Mint Fizz, 35
    Mr. 404, 11
    Nutcracker, 127
    Santa's Margarita, 117
    The Sidearm, 83
    Whiskey Sour, 147
lemon zest
    Alaska Cocktail, 64–65
    Americano, 162–163
    Aviation, 66–67
    Blue Moon Cocktail, 70–71

lemon zest (*continued*)
- Bobby Burns, 130–131
- Cancan, 39
- Dry Manhattan, 136–137
- French Martini, 24–25
- Improved Whiskey Cocktail, 155
- Lemon Drop, 30–31
- Maiden's Blush, 88–89
- Monte Carlo, 142–143
- Old Pal, 93
- Paper Plane, 146–147
- Rum Daisy, 58–59
- Sazerac, 135, 154–155
- Sidecar, 168–169
- The Sophisticate, 167
- Tahini Martini, 36–37
- Whiskey Sour, 147

Licor 43
- Apple Cream Pie, 43
- Bitter Blood Martini, 10–11
- Golden Vesper, 87
- The Last Word, 86–87
- The Monkey Gland, 85
- Santa's Margarita, 117
- Vanilla Love, 151

Lillet Blanc
- Aviation, 66–67
- Roaring '50s, 121
- Vesper, 98–99

lime juice
- The Bitter Spaniard, 119
- Coconut-Lime Daiquiri, 59
- Cosmopolitan, 20–21
- Daiquiri, 50–51
- Dr. B, 145
- Frothed and Fruity, 49
- Gin Daisy, 65
- Gin Fizz, 75
- Lime Cream Pie, 61

- Mai Tai, 52–53
- Margarita, 110–111
- Moscow Mule, 34–35
- Navy Grog, 51
- Rio Jengibre, 15
- Roman Punch, 169
- Tequila Mojito, 105
- Vodka Special, 31

lime zest
- Bourbon Mojito, 141
- Coconut-Lime Daiquiri Colada, 48–49
- El Diablo, 104–105
- Guadalajara, 109
- Moscow Mule, 34–35
- Naked and Famous, 114–115
- Pegu Club Cocktail, 67
- Pendennis Club, 95
- Rum Punch, 53
- Tropical Coconut Pie, 60–61

limoncello
- Amalfi Lemon Margarita, 102–103
- Italian Margarita, 103
- Lemon Drop, 30–31
Lychee-Mint Martini, 69

M

Madeira
- Bosom Caresser, 164–165

mango juice
- Frothed and Fruity, 49
- The Red Devil, 163

maraschino cherry syrup
- Luxardo Old Fashioned, 149
- Manhattan, 138–139

maraschino liqueur
- Aviation, 66
- Brooklyn, 134–135

- Improved Whiskey Cocktail, 155
- The Last Word, 86–87
- Smoked and Sassy, 116–117
- Venial Sin, 120–121
- Vodka Special, 31

Martinis
- Bitter Blood Martini, 10–11
- Cinnamon Toast Martini, 74–75
- Espresso Martini, 22–23
- French Martini, 24–25
- Gin Martini, 78–79
- Gingersnap Martini, 26–27
- Lychee-Mint Martini, 69
- Orange Martini, 94–95
- Pumpkin Spice Martini, 150–151
- Tahini Martini, 36–37
- Vodka Martini, 38–39

measuring cups, 7

mezcal
- Agave Fumar, 115
- Naked and Famous, 114–115
- Venial Sin, 120–121

milk
- Chai Slide, 17

mint
- Bourbon Mojito, 141
- Fog Cutter, 19
- Guadalajara, 109
- Lychee-Mint Martini, 69
- Mai Tai, 52–53
- Mint Fizz, 35
- Mint Julep, 140–141
- Mojito, 54–55
- Tequila Mojito, 105

muslin, 6

N

Negroni. *See also* Chocolate Negroni
nutmeg
    Buttered Rum, 44–45
    Santa's Margarita, 117

O

olives
    Gin Martini, 78–79
    Vodka Martini, 38–39
orange juice
    Roman Punch, 169
orange liqueur
    All Jammed Up, 25
    Biting Brandy, 165
    Bosom Caresser, 164–165
    Brando Russian, 16–17
    Brooklyn, 134–135
    Buttered Rum, 44–45
    Caribbean Christmas, 47
    Cosmopolitan, 20–21
    Damn-the-Weather Cocktail, 76–77
    Dr. B, 135
    Gin Fizz, 75
    Gingersnap Martini, 27
    Lemon Drop, 30–31
    Long Island Iced Tea, 32–33
    Mai Tai, 52–53
    Maiden's Blush, 88–89
    Margarita, 110–111
    Martinez, 90–91
    Parisian Blonde, 45
    Pegu Club Cocktail, 67
    Satan's Whiskers, 96–97
    Sidecar, 168–169
    Up and at 'Em, 73
orange zest
    Almond Joy, 124–125
    Bitter Blood Martini, 10–11
    Damn-the-Weather Cocktail, 76–77
    Eau de Tang, 129
    Gin and It, 81
    Golden Vesper, 87
    Hanky-Panky, 80–81
    Make Your Mark, 91
    Moscow's Sunny Side, 29
    Mr. 404, 11
    Negroni, 92–93
    Orange Martini, 94–95
    The Poet's Dream, 77
    Rio Jengibre, 15
    Satan's Whiskers, 96–97
    Sidecar, 168–169
    Up and at 'Em, 73
oranges
    Agave Spritz, 107
    The Bitter Spaniard, 119
    Harvey Wallbanger (High-End), 28–29
    Tequila Spritz, 119
orgeat syrup
    Fog Cutter, 19
    Inca, 71
    Mai Tai, 52–53
    Mint Fizz, 35
    Nutcracker, 127
    The Poet's Dream, 77
    Roman Punch, 169

P

paprika, smoked
    Agave Fumar, 115
peeler, Y-style, 7
pineapple
    Inca, 71
pineapple juice
    Bay Breeze, 21
    Bourbon Algonquin, 125
    Cabana Boy, 111
    Caribbean Cruise, 18–19
    Fog Cutter, 19
    French Martini, 24–25
    Rum Punch, 53
    Zombie, 55
pisco
    Fog Cutter, 19
Punt e Mes
    Chocolate Negroni, 72–73

R

raspberry jam
    All Jammed Up, 109
    The Bitter Spaniard, 119
rosemary
    The Sidearm, 83
rum
    Apple Cream Pie, 43
    Apple Pie Cocktail, 42–43
    Buttered Rum, 44–45
    Caribbean Christmas, 47
    Caribbean Cruise, 18–19
    Cinnamon Nut Bread, 46–47
    Coconut-Lime Daiquiri, 59
    Coconut-Lime Daiquiri Colada, 48–49
    Daiquiri, 50–51
    Fog Cutter, 19
    Frothed and Fruity, 49
    Lime Cream Pie, 61
    Long Island Iced Tea, 32–33
    Mai Tai, 52–53
    Mojito, 54–55
    Navy Grog, 51
    Parisian Blonde, 45
    Poker Cocktail, 56–57
    Roman Punch, 169
    Rum Daisy, 58–59

rum (*continued*)
    Rum Punch, 53
    Rumhattan, 57
    Sidecar, 168–169
    Tropical Coconut Pie, 60–61
    Up and at 'Em, 73
    Zombie, 55
rye. *See* Whiskey (rye)

S

scotch. *See* Whiskey (scotch)
sherry
    Fog Cutter, 19
    Inca, 71
sieves, 6
sparkling wine. *See* Wine, sparkling
sweet vermouth. *See* Vermouth, sweet

T

Tahini Martini, 36–37
tea
    Chai Slide, 17
tequila
    Agave Spritz, 107
    Amalfi Lemon Margarita, 102–103
    Cabana Boy, 111
    El Diablo, 104–105
    Guadalajara, 109
    Guadalajara Dos, 113
    Italian Margarita, 103
    La Rosita, 106–107
    Little Devil, 108–109
    Long Island Iced Tea, 32–33
    Margarita, 110–111
    Mexican Old Fashioned, 112–113
    The Red Devil, 163
    Roaring '50s, 121
    Santa's Margarita, 117
    Smoked and Sassy, 116–117
    Tequila Mojito, 105
    Tequila Spritz, 118–119
    Venial Sin, 120–121
thawing frozen cocktails, 2
thermometer, freezer, 7

V

vegetable juice
    Bloody Mary, 14–15
vermouth, dry
    Bourbon Algonquin, 125
    Brooklyn, 134–135
    Dry Manhattan, 136–137
    Exposition Cocktail, 99
    Gin Martini, 78–79
    Guadalajara Dos, 113
    Inca, 71
    Kiss in the Dark, 84–85
    La Rosita, 106–107
    Little Miss Sunshine, 37
    Orange Martini, 94–95
    Pegu Club Cocktail, 67
    Pendennis Club, 95
    The Poet's Dream, 77
    Satan's Whiskers, 97
    The Sophisticate, 167
    Vodka Martini, 38–39
vermouth, sweet. *See also* Punt e Mes
    Americano, 162–163
    Apple Pie Cocktail, 42–43
    Bijou, 68–69
    Biting Brandy, 165
    The Bitter Spaniard, 119
    Blood and Sand, 128–129
    Bobby Burns, 130–131
    Boulevardier, 132–133
    Carré Reprise, 171
    Corpse Reviver No. 1, 166–167
    Damn-the-Weather Cocktail, 76–77
    Dolce Vita, 139
    Dr. B, 145
    Drain the Swamp, 97
    Gin and It, 81
    Hanky-Panky, 80–81
    Highland Negroni, 157
    The Horse Thief, 82–83
    La Rosita, 106–107
    Make Your Mark, 91
    Manhattan, 138–139
    Martinez, 90–91
    Negroni, 92–93
    Orange Martini, 94–95
    Poker Cocktail, 56–57
    Rob Roy, 153
    Rumhattan, 57
    Rye San Martin Cocktail, 137
    Smoked and Sassy, 116–117
    The Sophisticate, 167
    The Southie, 153
    Sugar Daddy, 156–157
    Tequila Spritz, 118–119
    Upper East Side, 158–159
    Vieux Carré, 170–171
vodka
    All Jammed Up, 25
    Bay Breeze, 21
    Bitter Bastard, 27
    Bitter Blood Martini, 10–11
    Black (and White) Russian, 12–13
    Bloody Mary, 14–15
    Brando Russian, 16–17

Cancan, 39
Caribbean Cruise, 18–19
Chai Slide, 17
Coffee Cargo Cocktail, 23
Cosmopolitan, 20–21
Espresso Martini, 22–23
French Martini, 24–25
Ginger Screw, 33
Gingersnap Martini, 26–27
Golden Vesper, 87
Harvey Wallbanger (High-End), 28–29
Lemon Drop, 30–31
Little Miss Sunshine, 37
Long Island Iced Tea, 32–33
Mint Fizz, 35
Moscow Mule, 34–35
Moscow's Sunny Side, 29
Mr. 404, 11
Rio Jengibre, 15
Tahini Martini, 36–37
Vesper, 98–99
Vodka Martini, 38–39
Vodka Special, 31
White(-ish) Russian, 13

W

whiskey (bourbon)
    Almond Joy, 124–125
    Bacon Old Fashioned, 126–127
    Boulevardier, 132–133
    Bourbon Algonquin, 125
    Bourbon Mojito, 141
    Dolce Vita, 139
    Dr. B, 145
    Eau de Tang, 129
    The Love Bug, 133
    Make Your Mark, 91
    Manhattan, 138–139
    Mint Julep, 140–141
    Nutcracker, 127
    Old Fashioned, 144–145
    Paper Plane, 146–147
    Pumpkin Spice Martini, 150–151
    Vanilla Love, 151
    Whiskey Sour, 147
whiskey (rye)
    Blood and Sand, 128–129
    Brooklyn, 134–135
    Carré Reprise, 171
    Dolce Vita, 139
    Dr. B, 145
    Dry Manhattan, 136–137
    Eau de Tang, 129
    The Ginger Bear, 159
    Improved Whiskey Cocktail, 155
    Luxardo Old Fashioned, 149
    Manhattan, 138–139
    Monte Carlo, 142–143
    Old Fashioned, 144–145
    Philly Assault, 148–149
    Rye San Martin Cocktail, 137
    Sazerac, 135, 154–155
    Southern (Hemisphere) Comfort, 143
    Upper East Side, 158–159
    Vieux Carré, 170–171
whiskey (scotch)
    Bobby Burns, 130–131
    Highland Negroni, 157
    Rob Roy, 152–153
    The Southie, 153
    Sugar Daddy, 156–157
    Tropical Tartan, 131
wine, sparkling
    Agave Spritz, 107
    Bitter Bastard, 27
    Cancan, 39
    Harvey Wallbanger (High-End), 28–29
    The Sophisticate, 167

Y

yellow chartreuse
    Alaska Cocktail, 64–65
    Gin Daisy, 65
    Naked and Famous, 114–115
    Rum Daisy, 58–59
yogurt
    Lime Cream Pie, 61

ABOUT THE AUTHOR

J. M. Hirsch is a James Beard Award–winning writer and editor. He is the editorial director of Christopher Kimball's Milk Street and the former national food editor for the Associated Press. He lives in New Hampshire with his husband and two cats. He has written five books, including *Pour Me Another: 250 Ways to Find Your Favorite Drink*; *Shake Strain Done: Craft Cocktails at Home*; *High Flavor, Low Labor: Reinventing Weeknight Cooking*; and *Beating the Lunch Box Blues: Fresh Ideas for Lunches on the Go!* He has edited numerous others, including *Christopher Kimball's Milk Street: The New Home Cooking* and *Milk Street: Tuesday Nights*.